The Canoeist

Also by John Manuel

The Natural Traveler Along North Carolina's Coast

Hope Valley

For my father

The Canoeist
Copyright©2017 by John Manuel
All rights reserved

First Printing 2006

ISBN 978-0-9981112-2-3 (paperback)
ISBN 978-0-9981112-3-0 (electronic)

"In My Room"
Words and music by Brian Wilson and Gary Usher
©1964 Irving Music, Inc. All rights controlled and
administered by HAL LEONARD CORPORATION. All rights
reserved copyright renewed. Used by permission

Cover photo by John Manuel

Cover art by Dick Hill, Hill Studio
dickhillstudio.com

Book design by the Frogtown Bookmaker
Frogtownbookmaker.com

Published by Red Lodge Press
Redlodgepress.com

To Margaret,
So great to have you
in the book group.

John

The Canoeist

A Memoir

John Manuel

Red Lodge Press
Durham, North Carolina

Contents

Acknowledgments

Special thanks to A.J. Mayhew and her "Tuesday morning writing group" for their feedback in the writing of this book. Thanks also to Tim Barrus, a.k.a. Nasdijj, for recognizing the importance of the conflict between me and my father and insisting that this be made a central part of the book. Whatever misrepresentations Tim may have made of himself in his own writing, he encouraged me to speak the essential truth.

Note: This book is a memoir and, as such, depicts actual events to the best of my recollection. The names of the people in this book are real, except in instances such as summer camp at Keewaydin, where I cannot remember the actual names. These names are invented.

Chapter One
The Chagrin

Imagine you are canoeing in a fast-moving river and you come around a bend to see a line of head-high waves. You will never make it through without swamping your boat, but part way down, a midstream boulder offers temporary refuge. As the bow rises and falls through the waves, you angle toward the rock and circle into the eddy behind. There, in the calm, you bail water out of the canoe and still your beating heart. To complete the run, you must leave the eddy, paddle upstream into the current and turn your boat around. Instinct tells you to sit up straight, to keep the boat level. But the instant you turn sideways, the current rushing under the hull will grab the upright paddler and flip him over. Instead, you must lean downstream, reaching your paddle so far as to touch the water with your outstretched hand. Do this and you will ride the river to places you've never imagined.

* * *

I came back to our family home on the Chagrin River in Gates Mills, Ohio, to be with my father on his deathbed. Dad had been sick with cancer for five years, living under my mother's care. The last time I'd visited, he was gaunt and irritable, but still walking and eating. I was not prepared for how badly he'd deteriorated.

My mother leaned over the bed. "Here's Johnny," she said.

I hesitated at the door. Dad would want to brush down that shock of dark hair that stuck up like a cockscomb when he'd been in bed too long. I breathed in the sour smell of diapers, heard a faint groan. I entered the room.

On the pillow lay a shrunken head—sallow-skinned, cheeks collapsed—and a body so thin it barely rippled the bedcovers. Death had a hard twist on my father and was pulling him down through the mattress. *Should I touch him? How can I touch him?* I walked to the bed and lifted his hand, small and frail as a child's.

"How's it goin', Dad?"

Watery gray eyes turned my way and for an instant, I anticipated his rebuke—"How's it *goin'*?"—as if I had presented him with a bottle of cheap vermouth.

But he couldn't speak. A tear welled in his eye, something I'd never seen from my father. *Don't do this, Dad. Not now.* I let go of his hand and headed for the stuffed chair.

This was the way we usually did it—seated on opposite sides of the room, eyeing each other like serpent and prey. Dad would quiz me. I would answer, and wait for the inevitable put-down. About my job, my politics, my family. I would snort, look away. It was a dance we both knew well.

But when I looked up from the chair, Dad's forearm was still raised, fingers curled in the shape of my hand. I was frightened, ashamed. *He wants me to hold him. How can he want me to hold him?*

Mom was inspecting the forest of drug capsules on the nightstand. She could not save me. Sweat beaded on my forehead. I rose, took a step toward the bed. Dad's arm fell.

"Are you hungry?" Mom said. "I've made us some dinner."

We retreated to kitchen at the far end of the house, away from Dad, away from Death. Mom tied on an apron and stirred a pot of stew. Amazing that she could care for him, cook for herself and keep up with the house. The daughter of an alcoholic father with an unpredictable temper, my mother learned to take responsibility at an early age. In our family, she was the upholder of moral order and the peacemaker between Dad and us children. She was loyal to him through thirty-seven years of marriage and would keep him at home to the end.

I downed a spoonful of stew, as good as I remembered it.

"So none of the others could make it?" I asked.

Mom sighed. "Peter and Annie were here last weekend. Susie's off on some kayaking expedition in Oregon. I don't know how we'll reach her ..."

It suddenly struck me that Dad was going to die, probably within a day or two, and I would be the only one of his children present. Each of us kids had unresolved issues with Dad. We'd all broken his heart. Susie, the oldest, was the first to have casual sex, the first to get busted for pot. Since leaving for California in the 60s, she'd never been back for more than a week. Peter, my younger brother, was always defiant. He had bad table manners, dressed in laughably mismatched clothes, and expressed open disdain for Dad's beloved institutions—the Republican Party, the

3

Tavern Club, Yale University. Annie, the youngest, played the dutiful child until graduating from college, at which point she sold her IBM stock and gave the proceeds to some anarchosyndicalist cooperative in southern France.

But the tensions ran strongest between my father and me. I was the first-born son, the one he hoped would follow in his footsteps. And though I liked to think I had broken free, I was always circling back, hoping for those words of praise I was never going to hear.

* * *

Dad looked better in the morning. Daylight flooded the master bedroom through the picture window. Mom had propped him up on the pillow so he could see across the room. His eyes were resolute, unforgiving.

"Things are going pretty well at the magazine," I said. "I've been writing a series on canoeing."

He said nothing.

"Jackson's starting kindergarten. Allison's crawling all over the house."

Speak, Dad. Give me something. He drifted off to sleep.

Arranged on the recessed shelf above the bed were the keystones of my father's life—commendation of major from the Army Air Force, a portrait photograph from his days with the advertising agency, the gavel awarded him as Mayor of Gates Mills. When I was a child, these things bestowed such power on my father. Now they seemed to mock him in his sickness.

Dad woke and glanced around. "Water," he rasped.

Mom arrived as if on cue, cup and straw in hand. She sat on the bed and dipped the straw in the cup. Dad opened his mouth, and she dribbled the water in. "Would you like something more?

I'll get you some soup."

Mom left for the kitchen, and we were alone again. I leaned forward in the chair. "You faded out on me."

"Happens a lot," he said.

"What are you dreaming of when you go off like that?"

It was a bold question for me, but I wanted to know what a person thinks of when he is about to die.

"Canoeing. I dream I'm at Keewaydin. Right off the main dock."

I was surprised. Dad hadn't canoed in twenty years. And he hadn't been to Keewaydin since he was a boy.

"I didn't think you still cared about that," I said.

The old fire returned to his eyes. "Why wouldn't I?"

I retreated into silence. *Why wouldn't you? Because you always said I spent too much time at the river. Because you wouldn't even read the articles I wrote about canoeing. Because you never took my work seriously, not for the Conservation Foundation, not for the state, not for the magazine. Because you sneered at my choice of a home, my choice of a wife, the name of my son. Because I'm the canoeist, Dad. Not you.*

I stood up and walked down the hall into the brilliant light of the sunporch. Beyond the big picture window, the treetops swept down to the Chagrin River, dark and still in the late summer drought. This was the reason my father built this house, to gaze on this stretch of river. I had never wondered about the name "Chagrin"; always associated it with peace and beauty. Someone thought differently.

I shoved my hands in my pockets. What was it Dad was saying? Was canoeing just a dream or did it mean something more to him? I needed to know, because he was the one who put me in that boat and set me on the river. At 37, I still wasn't sure

5

where I was going, but I was finding my way. In so many ways, I was still that kid struggling to break free, and Dad was on the bank shouting, "Johnny, come back! Johnny, come back!"

* * *

The rain fell all night, and in the morning I could smell the river through the half-open window—wet earth with a hint of septic water. I jumped from my bed and peered into the valley to see the Chagrin swirling against the banks. Footsteps thumped up the stairs. Dad stuck his head through the door. "River's up. Want to run it?"

In an instant, I was dressed and headed down the hall. My six-year-old brother, Peter, stood at his bedroom door. He was too small for river running and would have to stay home. But nine-year-old Susie, older than me by a year, was dressed and ready to go. We ran down the stairs and into the garage where the boats hung from the ceiling.

We had two boats—a canoe and a Folbot. The canoe was a fourteen-foot-long Grumman, made of extra lightweight aluminum that Susie and I could carry. Technically, the canoe belonged to all three of us kids, but I considered it mine. Mom and Dad paddled the Folbot—a two-person kayak made of blue and gray canvas stretched over a wooden frame. Dad bought it based on an ad in *The New Yorker* that claimed the boat could be assembled in minutes and fit in the trunk of your car. He spent an entire weekend putting the thing together and would never take it apart again.

Mom and Dad loaded the boats on top of the Ford Country Squire and the four of us headed to Gates Mills and the river. Gates Mills is a wealthy suburb of east Cleveland. In colonial times and beyond, northern Ohio was part of the Western Reserve of Connecticut, and Gates Mills subsequently looks like an archetypal New England village, right down to the dam that diverted water to a mill. By the time I was born in 1950, the mill was long gone, but the dam remained. That was where our river trips began.

Mom and Dad lifted the boats off the car and eased them down the slippery path to the river's edge. This was a scary place for a child. Water thundered over the dam, and after a heavy rain, a reverse wave—a hydraulic—formed at the base. Dad said if you got stuck in a hydraulic, you would never get out. I stayed away from there.

While Mom and Dad slid into the Folbot, Susie and I, wearing our fat Mae West life preservers, eased into the canoe. Susie was bigger than me and got to paddle stern, but I comforted myself in thinking that I would eventually take that position.

"Are you kids ready?" Dad shouted.

With a wave of his hand, we pushed off the bank and left the everyday world behind.

Right away, there were rapids to negotiate—a pair of shallow ledges running diagonally across the river. The Folbot slid right over, its rubber bottom undulating like an inner tube. The canoe was another matter. Aluminum hulls are virtually indestructible, but they stick on rocks, even worse when they have a keel as ours did. If you think you're going to hit something, you need momentum to carry you through.

"Full speed ahead!" I called from the bow.

We were halfway over the second ledge when the canoe screeched to a halt. I pried my paddle against the bottom. "Push off."

The canoe wouldn't budge.

"Rock it."

Susie scowled. "I am rocking. Stop giving me orders."

We inched our way over the ledge, each ear-splitting jerk announcing our failure to the onlookers back at the dam. The canoe slid free, and we caught up to the Folbot.

"Next time, try running that V to the left," Dad said. "That's your deepest water."

I glanced to where he was pointing. Sure enough, there was a funnel of water distinct from the sharp edge we had come over. I could sense how the rock must dip down underneath, yielding a few extra inches of water. Now I knew what to look for.

We crossed under the Old Mill Road bridge and passed through the "back yard" of our small village. High on the east bank stood white, wood-framed Henry's Tavern where I got my grape soda and Bazooka bubblegum. St. Christopher's Episcopal Church stood on the west, its white steeple rising above the sycamores. St. Christopher's was Dad's church, the spiritual home of the WASPS who had settled Gates Mills and were still its exclusive residents. Our last name, Manuel, was suspiciously Latin, but Dad, with his high forehead, gray eyes, and ever-present tweed jacket, certainly had the Anglo-Saxon look.

Mom was an Irish Catholic. Her church—our church—was in a neighboring blue-collar town, where the congregation was peppered with Slavs, Poles, and Italians. Dad wouldn't set foot in that church, couldn't stand the sight of the black-veiled women fingering their rosaries. And yet he worshipped my mother. Despite his many prejudices, Dad saw most individuals for who they were.

"Look, children, the dogwoods are out!"

Mom was always pointing out the different trees along the bank, instructing us about their defining traits. Sycamores had the flakey trunks that turned bone white near the top. Beeches had smooth gray trunks and leaves that held on through the winter. My favorite trees were the hemlocks, evergreens that clung to the steep ravines feeding into the Chagrin. They were some of the oldest trees in the valley, and beneath their sheltering branches, the ground was always open, covered with a soft bed of needles.

As we rounded a bend, I glimpsed movement near the bank. Half a dozen turtles with heads like cormorants scrambled off a sandbar. I mentally scanned through my *Golden Book of Reptiles and Amphibians*.

"Duckbilled turtles!" I shouted.

Dad raised an eyebrow.

This was the thing about canoeing. If you were quiet, you could take animals by surprise. On trips down the Chagrin, we'd come upon hawks and herons and bullfrogs the size of catcher's mitts. The river was *their* world.

We came upon the Horvath's house hugging an eroding clay bank at a bend in the river. Sticking out of the bank was a black pipe that dumped a stinky, gray liquid right into the river. Dad said this was sewage from their septic tank. He warned us to steer clear. I asked if this was bad for the fish. He said it was.

"Can't anybody do something about it?"

Dad didn't answer. The Horvath's were his friends, just like the people who owned the steel mills in Cleveland that were polluting Lake Erie and the Cuyahoga River. He wasn't going to make a fuss about it. I figured it was just a matter of time before there was nothing left but carp and suckers.

"River Road Bridge coming up," Dad said. "Watch out for rocks."

Just beyond the bridge, the river slid into a long rapid. We followed the Folbot down the narrow V. I loved the feeling when the current started pushing you along, like an invisible hand under the hull. Trees become a blur, the air charged with sound and smell.

"Rock," I shouted. "Go left!"

I drew hard and felt Susie pry behind. The boat angled away. We scooted past the rock with room to spare.

Mom and Dad waited at the bottom. "Slow down, Jackson. You've got a ways to go."

Jackson was the nickname Dad used for me when he was feeling relaxed. He always seemed happy out on the river. There were just not enough Saturdays when the dogwoods were in bloom and the water was high.

* * *

The front door slammed. My father's footsteps thumped across the foyer. Dad was always in a bad mood when he came home from golf. I figured he sucked at the game and I wondered why he bothered playing.

"Where's Johnny?"

Mom answered from the sunporch. "I think he's upstairs with Peter."

Peter and I were in my room inserting firecrackers into a model B-25. Now in my early teens, I liked nothing better than blowing up airplanes. At the sound of Dad coming up the stairs, I ordered Peter out. He ran down the hall, but seeing Dad's shadow on the landing, turned back and ducked into the bathroom.

Dad loomed in the doorway.

"What are you doing?"

"Making an airplane."

"Where's Peter?"

"I don't know. In the bathroom."

His eyes dropped to my waist.

"Why is your fly down?"

I looked at my fly. I didn't know why it was down. Dad turned and banged on the bathroom door. "Come on out of there, Peter."

Peter cringed in the doorway.

"What were you and Johnny doing?"

"Nothing."

"Was Johnny playing with you?"

"We were playing Army."

Dad hustled him down the hall, came back and stood over me.

"Were you doing what I think you were doing?"

"What?"

"Fooling around."

I could tell this had something to do with sex, with touching my brother. He'd accused me of this before. But I had no interest in boys' penises. Why did he persist in believing that?

"We weren't doing anything wrong," I said.

"Get downstairs. You've got chores to do."

As his footsteps receded, I jumped onto my bed and cranked open the window. Dad had built a fire escape from the second-story bedrooms using pieces of pipe screwed into the siding. We weren't supposed to use it unless there was a fire, but it had become my way out of the house when I wanted to avoid being seen.

I scrambled to the ground, crawled past the sunporch, and darted into the garage. The pulleys creaked as I lowered the canoe to the floor. I hoisted the boat to my knees and duckwalked it to the edge of the woods. Wrapping the frayed bowline around my hand, I dragged it down the steep path, hull rattling over pebble and root. The spring woods sparkled with color—trillium, mayapples, trout lily, and violets. But there was no time to stop.

At the bottom of the hill, I carried the boat across River Road and dropped it in the Chagrin.

Out on the water I was my own master. One hard stroke sent the canoe surging ahead. A sweep spun it in circles. The slightest breeze could blow it off course, but down in the valley, there was rarely any wind.

I breathed in the smell of the Chagrin—growing plants, rotting leaves, wet loam—things living, dead, and in between, all mixed together in the olive green waters. Downstream, the river ran deep and slow half a mile to the dam. I was not in the mood for a crowd, so I headed upstream in the direction of the Tichy footbridge.

Most people in Gates Mills lived in colonial mansions with circular driveways and manicured lawns. The Tichys lived in a small house hidden in perpetual shadow of the Chagrin's steep, north-facing bank. The only access to that house was via a rickety wooden footbridge suspended over the river. We could see the footbridge from our hilltop home, and they, no doubt, could see our house, sunlight flashing off the big picture window.

I assumed the Tichys were poor because they lived across that bridge and swam in the river instead of the Hunt Club pool. They had two boys same age as me and my brother, but all comparisons stopped there. The Tichy boys were tough. They rode up and down River Road on their bikes, scowling at rich kids like me. If they saw me coming upstream in my canoe, they'd race onto the bridge. "Hey, kid, where'd you get that canoe? Kid, gimme a ride!" More than once, they tossed rocks at me as I hurried under the bridge. It was a gauntlet I had to run if I wanted to reach the wilder upstream portion of the Chagrin.

Beyond the footbridge, the river curved away from the road between banks thick with Joe-Pye weed. I slipped around the bend (no Tichy boys today) and headed for the gravel bar where the river reached the first rapid upstream of the dam. A blue heron stood in the shallows, searching for minnows and crayfish. He lifted his mattock-shaped head and fixed me with a sideways stare. *Please don't fly. Let me get close.*

The heron jumped into the air. I took aim with my paddle and fired a make-believe shot. Pow! He wheeled away, croaking like a dinosaur—*rah, rah, rah.*

I beached the canoe and stepped onto the cobbled surface of the gravel bar. The Chagrin is full of stones of all different shapes and colors, dragged down from Canada by a succession of glaciers. I picked up a piece of granite—bright pink flecked with gray—as smooth and round as a cueball. This one I'd like to have kept, but Mom said I had too many rocks.

Against the far bank, the river cut through the gravel bar. I knelt down and peered into the depths. Something bright caught my eye—a piece of metal fluttering in the current. It was attached to something black and hairy. A dog! Somebody's pet, probably fallen through the winter ice and drowned.

I thought of Katie Holmes, our next-door neighbor and my little sister Annie's best friend. Katie was over at our house every day, playing horse with Annie. They would set up jumps in the yard and trot around with hands held high, imaginary riders. I would sneak behind a tree and pop out like a stiff-legged zombie. Aarggh! They ran off screaming and laughing, "It's the ooly ghouly man!"

Earlier that summer, Katie went missing. She hadn't come home from day camp, a mile walk from the Gates Mills school. Word went out through the village, and I joined in the search, confident in my knowledge of the local woods that I'd find her sleeping beneath a hemlock. Like Prince Charming I would wake her with a gentle kiss and carry her back to her parents. But as the sun dropped low in the summer sky, my dream began to fade.

Searchers retraced Katie's path from the school. At one point, she would have had to cross a footbridge over the millstream that ran from the Chagrin through the elm-shaded grounds of the Hunt Club. That footbridge had no railing.

Mr. Holmes arrived home from work and borrowed a grappling hook from the Hunt Club Pool. As a crowd of onlookers gathered, he began raking the millstream. My friend Tom appeared.

"Do you think she's in there?" Tom said.

"Nah. He's been raking for half-an-hour."

The Gates Mills fire truck arrived, volunteers donning helmets and rubber boots. They stretched a rope across the millstream. Two firemen waded into the neck-deep water and, holding onto the rope, began walking along the bottom. They were nearing the footbridge when one of them stopped. I held my breath. The fireman handed off his helmet and ducked beneath the muddy surface. He rose with something in his arms, a girl in a white dress. Her arms were frozen straight up like a doll's, her mouth and eyes wide open. Katie.

Someone yelled. "Get the kids out of here!"

Like fireballs from an exploding star, we ran in all directions. I sprinted across the Hunt Club lawn, heading toward home. Halfway there, I stopped and knelt before the massive trunk of an elm tree. I put my hands on its rugged bark to assure myself that I wasn't dreaming. *Yes, this is real. Death is real. Katie's dead. We're all dead.*

* * *

Sunlight flickered off the water. I tossed the pink rock in the Chagrin and headed back to the canoe. The trip downriver passed in a blur. I carried the boat across River Road and dragged it up the hill. Dad was waiting in the back yard.

"Where've you been?"

"Down at the river."

"Doing what?"

"Fooling around."

The fight went out of his eyes. He stared at the canoe, wondering, I'm certain, how this craft that once brought us together now carried me away.

Chapter 2
Keewaydin

By mid-June, the Chagrin River was too low to paddle. The Tichy boys waded in the shallows, throwing their hooks and bobbers into the brown-tinged pools. They would be here all summer, while us rich kids went to "away camps" in New England, Canada, and the Rocky Mountains. At age fourteen, I was bound for Lake Temagami, Ontario, to attend Camp Keewaydin, the oldest wilderness canoe camp in North America and a Manuel family tradition.

On the built-in bookshelf in our wood-paneled living room, a tattered Keewaydin yearbook featured pictures of my father and his cabinmates posed in their longjohn swimsuits, hair slicked back and faces stern. Standing next to Dad was his twin brother, Bill, who died of leukemia in his twenties. Dad never mentioned Bill, I guessed for the same reason I didn't talk about Katie Holmes.

"Is this Lake Temagami, Dad?" I asked, as my father scribbled in his legal pad on the couch.

"Yep. Right off the main dock."

"It's big."

"A lot of paddling to get across."

The pages cracked as I turned them.

"How was the fishing?"

"Pretty good. Walleye and bass. Some northern pike."

I closed the cover and stared at the Keewaydin logo—a bull moose framed by a triad of paddles. I wouldn't care what I had to go through if I could see a moose. They were powerful, mysterious. To see a moose in the wild would mean there was still magic in the world. Had Dad seen one at Keewaydin?

"Other people saw them. I didn't."

The charter bus for Keewaydin left at nine at night, timed to reach the noon ferry from Temagami the following day. Station wagons arrived in the parking lot of Severance Mall and disgorged their cargo of adolescent boys. I gave Mom and Dad perfunctory hugs and slid my trunk into the belly of the bus.

As I stepped into the darkened interior, a couple of toughs called out. "Hey, look at this kid. Who is this dink?"

I froze. Why did they pick me out? Was it because I was skinny, freckled? Halfway back, my friend, Rusty, motioned me to the seat beside him. I hurried down the aisle, hoping not to get hit.

"Who are those guys?" I asked.

"I don't know. They must be from the West Side."

The door hissed close, and the engine rumbled to life. Out came the cigarettes and magazines. "Hey, Denny, throw me a Camel. None of that filtered shit." Smoke drifted up to the overhead lights. Rusty reached into his day bag and pulled out a *Playboy*.

"Have you seen Miss July? Check this out."

He held the magazine up and let the centerfold flop open. A long-legged blonde beckoned me to her bedside, turned just so to reveal the upward arc of her breasts. Blood rushed to my groin. Just then, something hit my sneakers—round, red, on fire.

The explosion sent my head ringing. I rocked forward with my hands over my ears. The bus driver slammed on the brakes and darkened the aisle.

"Next one of you motherfuckers lights a firecracker gets thrown off the bus. I don't care if it's in goddamn Saskatchewan. D'ya hear me?"

No one, not even the tough guys, made a sound. The driver sat down. The air brakes hissed. As the bus came up to speed, we eased open the windows, leaving behind a trail of cigarette smoke, gunpowder, and exhaust.

* * *

I awoke the next morning to a different world. Gone were the rolling pastures and leafy hardwoods of home, replaced by an untamed wall of evergreens. Groggy faces stared out in silence, the hubris of the previous night spent.

Thirteen hours after leaving Cleveland, we arrived in the town of Temagami and stopped in front of the ferry terminal on the shores of the eponymous lake. We stashed our cigarettes and girlie mags under the seats (both were banned at the camp on Devil's Island) and emerged blinking in the noonday sun.

"Get your trunks and take 'em over to the ferry," the driver said. "Anything you leave is mine."

The *Aubrey Cosens* was a relic from a bygone age, a passenger ferry with the graceful lines of a turn-of-the century steamship. We climbed up the gangway and settled into the wooden bench seats. A blast of the air horn sent us rushing to the rail. The ferry rumbled out the long, narrow inlet past sailboats at anchor and cabins with Canadian flags fluttering in the breeze.

As we turned onto the main stem of Lake Temagami, the water stretched to the horizon and a stiff wind blew my shirt against my chest. Keewaydin, the yearbook said, is an Ojibway Indian word meaning "northwest wind." The Indians considered this a good omen, a harbinger of clear skies. But the rolling whitecaps sent a chill down my spine. A boy could drown out there.

Twenty-two miles out of Temagami, the ferry slowed. Devil's Island emerged from the shadow of a low humped mountain. Green-roofed cabins peeked beneath the pines. Camp Keewaydin.

At the end of the dock, a tall man waited. He had steel blue eyes and a high, patrician forehead. As we walked down the gangway, he checked our names off a clipboard. "Wun'erful, wun'erful," he said in a sonorous baritone.

When we were all gather, he delivered his welcome speech. "My name is Howard Chivers. You can call me 'Chief.'"

I snickered to Rusty. "The head of my daycamp was called 'Chief.'"

He read off our cabin assignments—Rusty to Wabueno, me to Algonquin.

"Shit we're in different sections," I said. "That means we'll be on different trips."

Rusty sighed. "See you at dinner."

In the confines of the Algonquin cabin, I met the other members of my section. Kittredge lay in a lower bunk reading a science fiction paperback. He mumbled hello and went back to his book. Ned Speer bent over his trunk unpacking a pile of go-

19

kart magazines. He straightened up to reveal the slack jaw and long arms of a wrestler. "How ya doin', John?" I didn't normally go for jocks, but Ned seemed a friendly type. A short kid with a turned up nose and big lips stepped forward and offered his hand. "Sandy Dalton. Pleased to meet you," he said in his mother's voice. Here was one kid I could pull rank on. Chick Hancock was exactly my height, thin and freckled like me. His smile seemed genuine, his brown eyes attentive. He and I could definitely become friends. Then came the big guy. A head taller than I, dark stubble on his chiseled jaw, he pushed a shock of hair off his forehead. "Shephard."

Charlie Frasier, our resident counselor, looked at his clipboard and fixed me with a lop-sided grin.

"Manuel. Is that like manual labor?"

"Yeah, but with an 'e' instead of an 'a'."

Along with a counselor, each cabin was assigned a guide who planned and led the trips. The guides lived in their own cabins on the far side of the island. Many were locals of French-Canadian or Native American descent, including ours, Pete Morningstar.

Pete came around the first evening, a short, round-headed man with bright eyes and a quick smile. He squatted down before us on the cabin floor and unrolled a set of topographic maps. Amidst the pale green land mass were dozens of blue ovals. They had mysterious names like Wakimika, Obabika, and Timiskaming. Through the middle of a chain of these lakes, Morningstar had drawn a red line marking the path of our upcoming journey.

"Our first trip will be five days," he said. "We'll head up the north end of Temagami and portage into Red Squirrel. From there, we'll go through Jackpine, Chambers, and Ko Ko Ko. There'll be six portages, the longest one about three thousand yards."

I did a quick calculation. "Sir, that's over a mile-and-a-half!"

Morningstar looked up. "That's right, Manuel. It'll put some meat on those bones."

Shephard snorted. I retreated under his glare. We had kids like him at school—smart, athletic, good-looking—and still they had to put you down. I was going to have to shut up around him.

The next morning, we gathered in the meadow by the lodge to learn how to pack for our trip. Frasier laid out a sleeping bag, a pair of duffle bags, a green wooden box, and a canoe.

"Put your clothes on top of your sleeping bag and roll 'em up together with your ground cloth," he said. "Stuff that in your dufflebag and cinch it up with a tump line."

Frasier held up a twenty-foot-long leather strap with a headband in the middle. He wrapped it around a pair of dufflebags, tied a couple of knots to center the headband, and hoisted it onto his back.

"The bowman is responsible for carrying both his and his partner's dufflebags. The sternman carries the canoe."

Frasier moved on to the box, which he informed us was called a wannigan. He raised the lid to reveal cans of beef stew, peas, and evaporated milk standing four rows high and six across.

"A full wannigan weighs upwards of eighty pounds," Frasier said. "Some of you scrawny boys might have trouble getting it up. Manuel?"

I stepped forward and hoisted the wannigan off the ground. Frasier had to help me get it onto my back. As the tumpline stretched across my forehead, darts of pain shot through my neck. My head wobbled like a dashboard doll. I spun sideways and dropped the box.

Shephard laughed, "Way to go, Manuel."

"You'll get used to it," Frasier said. "They do get lighter as the trip goes on."

Keewaydin used only one kind of canoe, seventeen-foot-wood-and-canvas—the traditional canoe of the North Woods. I stared down the length of the upright hull. Cane seats. Ribs covered with layers of shellac. Frasier said the new ones weighed about eighty pounds, the older ones more than a hundred.

Frasier showed how to wrap a tump line around the center thwart for head support and tie in a pair of paddles to act as shoulder pads. He flipped the canoe overhead, where it sat like a giant billed cap, then lowered it back to the ground.

"Only the boys who paddle stern will carry a canoe," he said. "Who wants to try?"

Speer walked up, shaking his arms loose as if he were going into a wrestling match. He jerked the boat onto his thighs and flipped it overhead. His legs trembled from the weight of it. He threw it down and backed away.

"Gol, dang, that thing's heavy."

Shephard followed next. He got it up, of course, looking like Johnny Weismuller with his chest puffed out. He lowered it carefully to the ground and stepped aside.

Frasier eyed the rest of us. "You don't all have to try. We'll need four bowmen."

"I'll pass," Hancock said.

Kittredge shook his head. "Pass."

Dalton clucked and crossed his legs. "Surely, you jest?"

I hesitated. I had my own canoe at home, which I could carry over my head, but it was aluminum.

"I'll try," I said.

I stepped forward and reached out to close my hands around the gunwales. The boat looked impossibly long. I jerked upward and got the hull on my knees. I lunged for the center thwart and rolled the boat overhead. Halfway up, it stopped. I staggered sideways and dropped it. Bowman.

That evening, Frasier read the assignments: "Hancock, you're in the bow with Speer. Kittredge in the bow with Shephard. Dalton, you're with Morningstar. Manuel, you're with me." Tears welled in my eyes. Not only was I a bowman, I was stuck with a fucking counselor.

* * *

Dawn broke clear and windy. We lifted the canoes off the racks and carried them down to the water. Frasier placed the duffle bags in front of the center thwart and the wannigan behind. He wedged an ax behind the stern seat. I propped my fishing rod in the bow. Our whole world was packed into a seventeen-foot canoe.

Morningstar gave the signal and pushed off into the oncoming chop. "We've got us a Keewaydin," he called over his shoulder. "If your hat blows off, don't bother turning around."

I dug my paddle in the water. The hull rose and fell, sending a clap of spray to the sides. I took another stroke and another. The shoreline passed with agonizing slowness. At this rate, it would take all day to cross Temagami. I lowered my head and paddled harder.

"You're gonna wear yourself out like that," Frasier said. "Slow your stroke down. And don't just use your arms. Lean forward, plant the paddle and bring it back with your whole upper body."

I didn't need anybody to tell me how to paddle a canoe. But I followed Frasier's advice and felt the power of my torso.

"Now, turn your blade flat as you bring it forward. It'll cut the resistance to the wind."

The canoe gathered speed. As we passed the northern tip of Devil's Island, the shoreline fell away. Whitecaps winked all the way to the horizon. Clouds passed before the sun, changing the water from blue to gray and back to blue again.

Our fleet settled into a loose diamond, Morningstar in the lead, Frasier and I picking up the rear. I stared at a distant point and watched as it slowly merged with the shore. Another took its place, and another beyond that.

With nothing urgent to focus on, I lowered my gaze. I sung to myself the Beach Boys' latest hit. *There's a place where I can go and tell my secrets to, in my room, in my room.* Lulled by the creaking of the cane seats and the steady clap of waves, I fell into a trance.

"There's our portage."

Ahead the lake tapered into a cove. A faint gap in the understory of jackpine and birch marked the start of the path. We ran the canoes onto the rocks and began unloading.

"This one's about eight hundred yards," Morningstar said. "I'll leave my ax at the halfway mark. Bowmen, drop your wannigans there for your sternman to pick up and come back for your duffles."

One by one, the others hoisted their loads. I waited until everyone was gone, then duckwalked my wannigan over to a boulder. I squatted down, flipped the tump line overhead and rose on trembling legs. The rocks teetered beneath my feet.

With fearful steps, I made it onto solid ground and started up the incline. My neck muscles fired salvos of warning shots. *You are hurting yourself. Stop what you're doing.* I pulled forward on the tump line to ease the pressure. Step, step, step.

Mosquitoes rose from the damp leaf litter and danced before my face. I blew furiously to drive them away. They circled behind and sank their needles into my neck.

Finally, I'd had it. I pitched the wannigan on the ground and collapsed beside the trail. Why had my father sent me here? I was never going to make it.

At the sound of footsteps, I wiped away my tears. Hancock appeared heading back for his duffle bags.

"You O.K., Manuel?"

"Just taking a rest."

"Want some help with the wannigan?"

"I guess."

Hancock stepped behind me and lifted the box. I slipped the tump line over my forehead.

"How far to go?" I asked.

"Not much further. You can make it."

Dalton passed me on the way back to the put in. He'd made it to the halfway point without stopping. I shouldn't have been so quick to judge.

Finally, the wannigans appeared, piled like Christmas presents under a small hemlock tree. I pitched mine at the end of the row. My body seemed to rise off the ground. Dizzy, laughing, I glanced around for a witness. This must have been how Jesus felt when his spirit was freed of the cross.

Back at the put-in, the sagging weight of the dufflebags brought me back to earth. I shouldered my second load and trudged back up the trail. This time, I could lift my head enough to see into the forest. A tangled web of root and rock claimed the high ground. Down in the swales, wet bootprints pockmarked the muskeg, a spongy moss that could swallow a man up to his knees. A brilliant light flashed through the understory. There was Frasier sitting in our canoe.

"Get lost, Manuel?"

"Something like that."

I dumped the dufflebag in the canoe and took my seat. Morningstar gave a nod, and we pushed off into new water.

Red Squirrel Lake was smaller and wilder than Temagami. There were no cabins here, no boats save our own. We fanned out four abreast, our canoes flying across the ruffled surface.

Morningstar began to sing in a high clear voice: "*Down de way where de nights are gay and de sun shines daily on de mountaintop ...*"

Frasier picked up the chorus, and soon we were all singing, transformed from eight struggling souls to something new, something whole—a tribe.

The campsite stood on the far shore atop a sloping slab of granite. We hauled our gear up the incline and scanned the level ground. A circle of rocks marked previous groups' campfires.

"Put the wannigans by the fire rings and get your tents set up," Morningstar said. "Looks like the last crew left their tent poles, so you won't need to cut any new ones."

Hancock, Speer, and I claimed a rectangular patch of bare ground and unfolded the heavy canvas tent. We fastened two pairs of tent poles together with tump lines and spread them apart to make an X. Speer ran a fifth pole through the roof sleeve and hung it in the notches. With the canvas sides anchored to nearby rocks, our little home was ready.

Inside, the tent was dark and musty. "I got this side," Speer said.

Hancock claimed the other. I was happy to be in the middle, buffered from the unknown by my friends. We unrolled our sleeping bags and stacked our clothes at one end to make pillows. Speer brought out a magazine.

"Do you have a go-kart, Ned?" I asked.

"Heck, yeah. Six-horsepower Carter."

"My parents said they might buy me one for Christmas," I lied. "What kind do you think I should get?"

Speer flipped through the pages and stabbed with his finger. "Turbo kart. Fucker'll go thirty miles an hour."

Hancock was doing his summer reading, *Catcher in the Rye*. "You got a go-kart, Chick?"

"Nope. A bicycle."

"Ten-speed?"

"Just a regular one."

I felt humbled by Hancock's honesty. Funny how he seemed stronger even than Speer.

"I'm not sure my parents would get me that turbo model," I said. "Maybe the regular one."

The smell of woodsmoke drifted through the mosquito netting. We grabbed our mess kits and gathered around the fire, where a pot of beef stew simmered on the irons.

"All right!" I said. "My mom makes beef stew."

Shephard put on a high voice. "Alright, my mom makes beef stew."

"Knock it off, Shephard," Morningstar said.

After dinner, I carried my messkit down to the shore and scrubbed it clean. As the leftovers sank, a small fish appeared out of the depths and snatched them up. I stared at the lake, the pale light of evening held in the mirrored surface.

I walked back to the fire ring where Frasier sat smoking a cigar. "Sir, can I take the canoe out to fish?"

Frasier stared out at the lake.

"You sure can you handle it alone?" he said.

"Yes, sir, I have my own canoe at home."

"Be back by dark," he said.

Without the heavy gear, the canoe skimmed across the surface. I took gentle strokes, soundless save for the rhythmic hiss of the hull as it cleaved the water. I stopped to rig my rod. Dad said a Daredevil should work up here. I tied on the red-and-white spoon and cast it out to stern. Propping the rod against my thigh, I resumed paddling, following a course parallel to shore where the mirrored pines met the darkening sky.

The cry came from somewhere across the lake, a high tremulous laugh. Woo, woo, woo, woo. My heart raced. *What is that? A loon. Must be a loon.* As suddenly as it rose, the crying stopped, the last note echoing off the far shore. I looked back toward camp, wondering if the others had heard it.

Just then, my rod jumped. I grabbed the reel as it flew over the side. The line screamed against the drag. Whatever this was, it was big. *Please don't break. Please don't break.* The line stopped moving. Had I lost him? I cranked in. A dark shape emerged beside the boat. Whap! The fish slapped the hull and charged away. A northern pike! I had only seen pictures of them in magazines, but as I hauled him in a second time, the trademark head emerged—long, flat snout, teeth like a barracuda. He only fit halfway into my net, but I managed to lift him into the canoe, where he flopped twice and lay still.

The stars were out by the time I made it back to camp. I carried the fish into the firelight where Frasier and Morningstar were leaned back against a log.

"Holy shit, where'd you catch that thing?" Frasier said.

"About halfway around the lake. Right by a fallen tree."

"Whad' you catch him on?"

"Daredevil."

Morningstar took the fish by the gill. "Nice. About eight pounds. Are you going to eat him?"

I shrugged. "I'm kinda stuffed."

"Clean him up, and we'll see if anyone's interested."

Word of my catch spread through camp. One by one, my mates emerged from their tents. As Dalton leaned in, I jerked the toothsome head upward. "Ew, get that thing away from me!"

I took the fish down to the shore and pulled out my sheath knife. Shephard appeared at my shoulder.

"Where'd you catch that?"

"Out past that point. He took a Daredevil."

No comment. Shephard wouldn't know a Daredevil from a Hula Popper. I shoved the knife into the pike's anus and ran it up the belly. The guts pulled out easy.

* * *

The dining lodge echoed with the chatter of 120 boys bragging about their first trip. Rusty sat next to me, wolfing down his fried chicken.

"Guess what? My canoe weighs a hundred pounds," he said. "Buck says it's one of the heaviest ones in camp." Rusty was a sternman and, so he claimed, the strongest kid in his section.

"Yeah?" We had a three-thousand-yard portage," I countered. "Try carrying an eighty-pound wannigan over that!"

I neglected to mention that my wannigan was nearly empty when we crossed that portage. Nor did I say that Morningstar estimated my pike to be eight pounds, not ten.

After lunch, Chief rose to welcome us back. "Wun'erful, wun'erful. So good to see everyone."

He announced there would be mail in the post office and that any "CARE" packages from home with candy and the like were to be turned over to your counselor for equal distribution. Then, Chief's Number Two man, Roy Walters, got up to read the Major League baseball scores from the previous week. Apparently, this was a tradition, as the older campers booed or cheered the results. I didn't much care. It was 1964, and the Cleveland Indians sucked.

At the post office, I received two letters from Mom describing the weather at home and reminding me that she and Dad would soon be headed for France. There was nothing from Dad, but I didn't think much about it. Fathers didn't write to their sons.

* * *

Our second journey was a seven-day trip through the Obabika-Wakimika circuit. We headed north again on Lake Temagami, west across Diamond, and south into Lake Wakimika.

Two weeks had passed, and I had yet to see a moose. I scanned the shoreline around every bend. Nothing but trees and more trees. On the second morning, we entered the serpentine channel of the Wakimika River. Memories of the wildlife along the Chagrin gave me hope that we might see something here. I called to Morningstar in a stage whisper.

"Sir, is there any chance we might see a moose?"

"It's possible. They like to wade out and feed on the aquatic grasses. Have to be quiet, though."

Along the river bottom, mats of yellow-green grass wavered with the current.

"Hey, guys, Pete says we might see something if we're quiet," I said.

In the canoe beside me, Dalton nicked his paddle against the gunwale at the end of each stroke. I fixed him with an angry stare. He clucked and rolled his eyes.

The miles passed without a sighting. Each bend brought another empty sandbar, another wall of trees. At length, the river opened onto the wide expanse of Obabika Lake. I dropped my head and settled into the old, familiar mantra. Stroke, stroke, stroke.

Day three was a rest day, a chance to sleep late and explore our surroundings. Frasier led a group of us across the lake to a rocky bluff that was perfect for diving. The outcropping offered three platforms of varying height. We started at the lowest level, about twelve feet.

"Go, Hancock," I said.

He clutched his bare shoulders. "I'm not going first. You go."

Diving was something I loved. I spent hours launching myself off the board at the Hunt Club, doing flips, can openers, and watermelons. Curling my toes around the edge of the granite, I leapt out, puffing my chest and spreading my wings. I hit the water and surfaced with a triumphal yell.

Speer and Shephard dove in behind me. Hancock jumped feet first. We climbed up to the next level, something close to twenty feet.

The water delivered a hard slap to the top of my head. I shook it off and swam slowly to shore. After another dive from that height, I decided to go to the top.

"I'm not going up there," Hancock said.

Speer frowned. "I'll jump, but I ain't diving."

The three of us huddled at the top of the outcropping.

"Man, I'll bet we're fifty feet up," Speer said.

Shephard shook his head. "I'd say it's closer to thirty."

I pointed out the campsite across the lake and the ant-like figures of Dalton and Kittredge. Fraiser waited in his canoe. "You guys gonna go?"

Speer backed away. "This is too high for me."

Shephard turned to me. "You gonna do it?"

I peered over the edge, imagined the dizzying drop through the air, the punch of the water. I could barely lift a full wannigan. I couldn't carry a wood-and-canvas canoe. But I could leap off a cliff, hollering like Tarzan all the way down.

* * *

Back at base camp, we gathered in the dining hall. Rusty was full of his usual post-trip bravado. His canoe had added another ten pounds, and his portages ran on for miles. Roy Waters got up and read the baseball scores; then he added some unexpected news.

"Yesterday, two of our Navy destroyers were attacked by North Vietnamese gunboats in a place called the Gulf of Tonkin. The destroyers sank four of these boats, so the score was U.S.A, four, North Vietnam, zero."

We all cheered. Who was North Vietnam and why would they think they could beat the U.S. Navy?

After lunch, Rusty invited me back to his cabin where he produced a small wooden canoe.

"Check it out. Buck carved it for me."

Buck Lejamb was Rusty's French-Canadian guide and, if I was to believe it, his second father. I turned the boat over in my hands. "Reminds me of *Paddle to the Sea*."

Paddle to the Sea was my favorite book, a richly illustrated story about an Indian boy who carves a miniature canoe and paddler and sets it on a snow bank above Lake Nipigon. The snow melts and launches the canoeist on a torturous journey through the Great Lakes, the St. Lawrence River, and finally the Atlantic Ocean. Each time the canoeist is washed ashore or trapped in a log jam, someone finds him and sets him back on his journey.

I would have loved for somebody to carve me a toy canoe, but whatever it took to attract that kind of gift, I didn't have it. I had a certain wariness around men. They sensed it and kept their distance. I handed Rusty back the canoe.

By then, we'd been at camp a full month. We'd both filled out, our necks thick with trapezius muscles, arms sinewy and long. Rusty could still pin me in spontaneous wrestling matches, but I wasn't the pushover I used to be.

The next trip, our last, would be a full two weeks. As Morningstar described our upcoming journey, I traced the route on my own set of topo maps purchased at the camp store.

"We'll head up Temagami, cross Lady Evelyn Lake and paddle up the Lady Evelyn River," he said.

Great. Paddle upstream against the current.

"Couple of short portages gets us into the Grays River. Then, we've got a four-thousand-yarder into Lake Makobe."

Shit, a two-mile portage. That was enough to make me cry, but it got us into a lake and, wonder of wonders, a river that drained out of the lake and that we would run downstream.

"Most summers, the Makobe's too shallow to run," Pete said. "But we've had enough rain that it should be passable. It's a wild river. No Keewaydin group's run it in years."

We left the next morning under bright sun. A warm wind, a Wabueno, blew out of the south, pushing us along at a steady pace. *Screw the Keewaydin. I'll take a Wabueno any time.*

We set up camp on a rocky island in the middle of Lady Evelyn Lake with a three-hundred-and-sixty-degree view. Earlier in the afternoon, I'd seen the horsetails streaming out from the horizon. Now they covered half the sky. As the sun dropped behind Maple Mountain, the feathery clouds lit up from below.

"Look at that," I breathed. "They're changing from scarlet to pink."

"That one over there is purple."

Frasier sniffed. "Enjoy it while you can. We'll pay the price tomorrow."

I woke the next morning to a downpour. We ate our oatmeal under the fly, rain water streaming off the edges. I dreaded getting in the canoe, the cold rubber rain suit plastered to my naked arms and legs. My canvas sneakers were quickly soaked.

We paddled in the rain all day, struggling upstream against the rising current of the Lady Evelyn River. Every few miles, we had to portage around rapids. The footing was slick. Branches drooped across the path, wiping their cold wet hands across my face.

As soon as we made camp, we crawled into our tents and got out of our wet clothes. We lit candles and swatted at the mosquitos that made it through the tears in the netting. Hancock reached in his dufflebag and produced a small cookie tin. "Got a little present for you guys."

Speer lit up. "Chocolate chip! I thought Chief said we had to give those to our counselor?"

"Screw Chief," Hancock said. "Guy needs an enema."

"Wun'erful, wun'erful," I said.

At noon the next day, we reached the dreaded portage into Makobe Lake. A month ago, I would have had to set the fully loaded wannagin on a boulder just to get underneath it. Now, I lifted the box straight off the ground and swung it onto my back.

The portage into Makobe was notorious for its muskeg. In a dry summer, the mossy ground might support a man's weight, but after two days of rain, it was like quicksand. As I followed the path to the low ground, I saw a canoeist sunk to his knees—Shephard.

"Shit! Goddamn muskeg!"

"You want me to help you, Shep?" I said.

"I can't fucking move."

"Here, I'll hold the boat up."

I eased my wannigan to the ground and raised the canoe off Shephard's shoulders. He pulled his legs out of the muck and shook loose his neck and arms.

"Looks like dry ground just ahead," I said. "You want to drag the boat?"

"That's O.K. I can handle it."

I waited to make sure Shephard could walk, then picked up my wannigan and slogged on ahead. Step by step, yard by yard, we all made it across the portage.

As we paddled into Makobe Lake, the clouds parted to reveal a fractured window of blue. The window closed as quickly as it opened, but the momentary flash gave me hope. The eye of God winking.

Morningstar paused in the middle of the lake and scanned his topo map. He pointed to a barely perceptible break in the wooded shoreline. "That should be the outlet," he said.

We'd been warned that the headwaters of the Makobe River were likely to be shallow. What we found was little more than a boulder-strewn path disappearing into the jackpines. A chorus of groans erupted from the group. But something about the river looked right to me. Wilderness.

We set up camp where the river left the lake. After dinner, I got out my fishing rod and tied on a little Mepps spinner. At the sudden tug, I jerked back and sent the fish sailing through the air. It landed at my feet, a speckled trout barely six inches long. I picked it up and examined the lavender bulls-eyes with the bright red centers. What they lacked in size, they made up for in beauty. I removed the hook and put the brookie back in the stream. He disappeared in a flash, his mottled backside becoming one with the rocky bottom.

At first light, we set our canoes into the river. Morningstar led the way, prying off the bottom with his paddle. Within minutes, he was aground. We stepped out of the canoes and waded until we reached deep water, paddled another dozen yards, got out and waded.

By mid-afternoon, we'd only covered a few miles. Dalton slogged along the bottom kicking up rocks. I was hoping we might surprise a mink or beaver, but as much noise as he was making, we'd be lucky to see a bluejay.

Morningstar began searching for a campsite and settled on a narrow shelf by the water's edge. As I prowled the shoreline looking for firewood, I came upon a set of cloven hoofprints pressed into the sand. They were still filling with water.

I scanned the forest for the giant ears cupped to take in the sound of the pursuer. I strode forward, pushing aside branches of hemlock and alder. He was here, I was certain. Just over the next ridge.

That night, I lingered by the water while cleaning my messkit. Trees across the river faded to black. Stars came out in the narrow band of sky. When I could no longer tell the water from the land, I retreated.

In my dreams, a moose stalked the forest behind our tent. He watched me with dark all-knowing eyes, always just out of reach.

"Awfully quiet this morning," Frasier said as I loaded the canoe.

"Yes, sir. Hoping we might see something."

Frasier chuckled. "You're always hoping, Manuel."

The Makobe was deep enough now that we could paddle without running aground. A heavy mist hung over the water, jackpines rising above like dark steeples. The eerie landscape beckoned us to silence. We moved in single file with the gentlest of strokes, dripping paddles beading the surface with a sound like rosaries poured from hand to hand.

The sun burned the mist away, revealing banks thick with blueberries. Morningstar raised his hand. Something was in the bushes.

All summer long, we'd paddled along shorelines as immutable as paintings. Leaves might flutter in the afternoon breeze. A kingfisher might fly from its perch. But we'd never seen anything like this.

With silent strokes, we closed the distance—twenty yards, fifteen …Dalton nicked his gunwale, and the bushes exploded. The bear rose on her hind legs, a Goliath sprung from the earth. She sized us up with the eyes of a dog, raised her paws to her chest. Branches quivered as a pair of cubs hustled away, their hind ends yo-yo-ing into the forest. She turned back to check on her cubs, froze us with a withering huff, dropped to the ground and was gone.

* * *

By week's end, we were on the *Aubrey Cosens,* heading back to the mainland. I leaned against the railing, topo maps rolled under my arm. Boys crowded the tables on the top deck, playing cards, talking loud. As we turned into the northeast arm of Temagami, our ferry overtook a pod of canoes. If not for the flash of the paddles, I'd have thought the boats were standing still. For a moment, it struck me as foolish to travel like that—yard by yard across a vast, watery plain. But you didn't get tested by riding the ferry. Dad knew that much. That's why he sent me here.

There's a lot to be said for the perseverance of putting one stroke after another, mile after mile for weeks on end. It builds strength, of course, but it's also deeply meditative. Your life slows down when you pass through the world at just a few miles an hour. There would be periods in my life when I wanted to experience that again. But after eight weeks at Keewaydin, with the mid-1960s in full swing, I wanted to move faster.

Chapter 3
The Lost

I came to the nation's capital in 1972 without a canoe, looking for a job and some meaning in my life. Jimi Hendrix was dead, the Vietnam War was unraveling, and Richard Nixon was president. Cynicism reigned. But I was fresh out of Yale and hoped to get a job with one of the new non-profit agencies that were pushing for change in environmental policy, consumer protection, or social justice.

The summer of 1972 was a heady time in D.C. Nixon may have ruled the White House, but he seemed vulnerable in the upcoming presidential election. D.C. was thick with Democrats, and we strolled around town as if we owned it.

I rented a basement apartment on Capitol Hill with three former college roommates. They all held jobs in the federal government, but I had no interest in joining the bureaucracy. I wanted a job where I could dress in blue jeans and lob spitballs at Republicans. Ralph Nader seemed to offer an answer to my prayers. Leading up to the 1972 elections, Nader was hiring writers and editors to produce reports on every member of Congress, including their voting records, financial support, and ranking by environmental and consumer groups. I was too late to get in on the writing and had to settle for an editing position. Checking for proper punctuation wasn't the best use of my Yale education, but I enjoyed being associated with the man who was stripping the emperors of their clothes.

The honeymoon lasted about six months. Nader paid slave wages, expecting us to emulate his monkish lifestyle—no car, no house, no free time. He seemed to find fault with everything produced in America, and though I didn't work for that part of his organization, his self-proclaimed status as the nation's consumer advocate started to bug me. The hotdogs I craved were poison, Dad's perfectly good Corvair "unsafe at any speed." When he went after "dangerous toys," I lost all patience. If you were dumb enough to put a jet plane in your mouth, you deserved to bleed.

One day, Nader ordered the Congress Project staff down to the Federal Trade Commission to demonstrate for some upcoming ruling on toy safety. He gave me a sign that read "Sharp Edges Make Me Cry" and had me walk in circles around the building. I handed in my resignation the next day.

The Yellow Pages listed two enticing names under "Non-Profit Organizations"— the American Rivers Council and the Environmental Defense Fund, both at 801 Pennsylvania Avenue. I climbed the stairs, resume in hand, anticipating a posh suite buzzing with legions of the faithful. Instead, I opened the door to a one-room office lit by the harsh glare of fluorescent lights. Two guys sat behind desks piled high with newspaper clippings.

"I don't have any jobs right now," said the guy from the American Rivers Council. "But if you'd like to do some volunteer work, something might open up."

"That's O.K. Can you direct me to the Environmental Defense Fund?"

"That would be him."

Hard up for cash, I hired on as a sheetrocker with Grant Doe Construction Company. Grant's specialty was buying up rowhouses from poor blacks on Capitol Hill, renovating them, and selling them at top dollar to a bunch of puffed-up Congressional staffers. My job was to follow after Hassan, the "mud man," and sand down the plaster seams. My goal was to create a perfectly blank wall.

Much as I hated my job, I loved living in the District. Saturday mornings, I played touch football on the lawn in front of the Lincoln Memorial. I was plenty fast, and if I caught a pass in the open, no one could catch me, not even the black guys. The town was full of beautiful women and fun places to take them. Carol liked bluegrass at the Birchmere. Renate preferred biking in Rock Creek Park.

I was stunned when Nixon got reelected in the fall, but no sooner was he back on his throne than the castle walls began to crumble. *The Post* got the scoop on the Watergate break-in, and Nixon's henchmen started to sing. Calls rang out for Tricky Dick to resign. Someone organized a "Honk If You Think He's Guilty" rally downtown. I raced over from work in my dirt-stained Capri and drove in circles around the White House, horn blaring, long hair streaming out the window.

With all the excitement in the District, it was easy to forget about nature. But water was never far away. The Potomac ran right through the center of town, more a reflecting pool there than a living, breathing force. But fifteen miles upstream in a place called Great Falls, it crashed over the fall line in a series of spectacular drops.

On a crisp fall afternoon, I stood on the Maryland side of the falls, tracing the frothy current as it boiled around boulders and thundered over ledges. The falls looked too dangerous to run in a canoe, but downstream, the river flowed through a gorge that looked doable. All I needed was a boat.

Mid-December, I drove back to Cleveland to celebrate Christmas with my family. Dad was glad to see me. He took me down to the Tavern Club for the annual Christmas party. There was Asa Shiverick with his lighted bow tie and Frat Vilas in his green sport jacket. "He's just out of Yale," Dad said to Frat.

On the ride home, the conversation turned my job with Grant Doe Construction Co.

"I sent you to college so you could sand sheetrock?" Dad said.

"Don't worry, Dad. It's not forever."

"Stuey Harrison said he might have something down at Cleveland Cliffs. Why don't you give him a call?"

"Cleveland Cliffs? They're the ones dumping crap into Lake Erie!"

Dad scoffed. "You and Nader."

I wanted to know if Dad was going let me take the canoe back to Washington. We'd never discussed whose boat it was. Dad bought it for all of us, but I was the only one who used it anymore. I asked him the question. He looked away.

"Fine. I'm taking it," I said.

* * *

As soon as the weather warmed, I drove with the boat out to Great Falls. There was a parking lot by the old C&O canal and a path leading down to the river. People were standing on the rocks at the big bend below the Madeira School, watching a group of kayakers surf the rapids. I was jealous of this new breed of paddler. They could bob through the waves without taking water and roll upright after a spill. But I figured with a little practice, I could do almost anything they could.

My plan was to put in at the top of the bend, make a quick run through the rapids, then turn around and try a little of that surfing. I felt a twinge of fear putting my boat in the water. The current looked powerful—stronger than anything else I'd ever paddled. But I could see only one serious obstacle, a large rock in the middle of the bend. There was plenty of room on either side. I'd decide which way to go once I was out on the water.

The instant I left shore, the current grabbed my boat and swept me toward midstream. I was moving so fast I couldn't gauge which side of the rock to shoot for. At the last second, I chose the inside passage. Too late. The boat clanged against the rock, yawed to one side and took on water. I threw myself onto the opposite gunwale and brought the canoe back to level.

The kayakers watched stone-faced as I paddled through the next rapid. I angled toward shore, trying to act nonchalant. One of the kayakers broke free of the group and peeled in beside me.

"You all right, buddy?"

"Yeah, I'm fine."

"I can't believe you're out here with no life preserver. That's exactly how people drown."

"I was just running that one rapid."

"One is all it takes."

I needed to get away from this guy, but he wouldn't let go of my boat. He eyed the water-filled hull.

"You ought to get some flotation for this thing."

"Flotation?"

"A styrofoam block, an air bag, something to keep your boat on top of the water when you swamp like that. We've already had four drownings out here, and the Park Service has threatened to close the river if we have any more."

Fuck you, asshole. You and your dick-nosed kayak. He was right, of course. This canoe was a joke. I was a joke. I couldn't run a simple rapid without hitting a rock. I hauled the canoe out of the water and, trying to avoid the accusing stares of the bystanders, humped it back to the car.

* * *

A few weeks later, my high school friend, Stephen, called from Cleveland. "Hey, Johnny boy, I hear you're hanging out with a bunch of your Yale buddies. How's about letting me stay in your apartment for a few weeks while I look for work?"

Stephen was a jokester with a reckless streak that both enticed and scared me. Before he arrived at my high school, I was a straight-A student, prone to making snide remarks under my breath, but never doing anything that would compromise my grades. Here came Stephen, laughing out loud, urging me to do the same.

Stephen paid rapt attention to the teachers he respected and skewered the ones he didn't. Sleepy Phil, an alcoholic American history teacher well past retirement age, was among the latter. Phil liked to lace his lectures with anecdotes about the derivation of modern terms—"three sheets to the wind", "shake a leg"— which we considered to be of dubious authenticity. Stephen would wait for him to finish, then pronounce loud enough for the whole back row to hear, "Ah, ya' lyin' bag of shit!" I never laughed so hard. And my grades never sank so low.

"There's only supposed to be three of us in this apartment," I said. "I'm sleeping on the couch, and I'm not sure my roommates want anybody else."

"Just tell 'em I've got some dynamite weed."

As I predicted, Stephen's stay lasted months, not weeks. He couldn't find the job he wanted with the American Friends Service Committee and ended up painting houses, another B.A. with blistered hands. Stephen slept in the living room on the couch next to mine. He was reading a lot of Carlos Casteneda, and we'd lie awake at night, talking about power spots and flying spirits.

My roommates tolerated the newly cramped living conditions, but they were less than amused with Stephen's insistence upon shifting their political discussions to a spiritual level.

"You guys gotta understand that Nixon can't escape his own karma. Babba Ram Dass says ..."

"Man, you are so full of shit!"

One night, a downpour hit the D.C. area. The pipes in our basement apartment backed up, sending raw sewage into the living room. The landlord was called, discovered five people in his apartment, and ordered me and Stephen out.

We were glad to be on our own. Stephen and I rented an apartment on East Capitol Street underneath the shady elms. We bought a used couch and chair and a pair of double mattresses. We made grocery lists, me agreeing to Stephen's request for soybeans and tofu. Then, we started to clash. We disagreed over who spent how much money for what. We argued about how long Stephen was gone with my car and when he promised to be back. Some days, we could hardly stand the sight of each other. Other days, we got along like old times.

Tired of painting houses, Stephen took a job as an elevator boy at the Rayburn Building, 5 pm to midnight. He invited me to come over some nights after work and sit out on the Capitol steps. We lit up a joint, looked over the city, and mused about the future.

"You ought to run for office, John. You've got the looks. You make friends easily."

"Nah. Could you see me putting on a suit and asking people like my dad for money? 'Hey, man, I *really* need your support! Asshole!'"

Stephen laughed. "Your dad's not a bad guy. He's got more integrity than most men I know."

It made me nervous to hear Stephen talk like that. It was so much easier when I could make fun of Dad and not think about my own situation.

The sheetrocking job had become torture. I couldn't stand the thought of staring at yet another blank wall, rubbing that sandpaper back and forth. By the end of the day, I'd be covered in white dust, a ghost condemned to walk the streets.

One day, I came across an article in the *Washington Post* about a place called the Lost River. "Listen to this, Stephen. 'The Lost River meanders through the West Virginia countryside before literally disappearing into the side of a mountain. It emerges several miles downstream ...'"

"Hey, I've got a buddy who lives in Lost River," Stephen interjected. "He grows some killer weed."

On a Friday afternoon in April, we loaded the canoe on the Capri and headed for the Appalachian Mountains. Ludwig was waiting for us, joint in hand, on the front porch of the spruce-shaded bungalow he shared with his senile father. Ludwig looked like a Rubens satyr, flaming red hair and goatee. He plied us with a constant supply of marijuana, which he claimed to have planted and harvested along the West Virginia roadsides. "Pops," confined to the back bedroom, was apparently too far gone to know what was going on.

"Turn that goddamn radio down!" Ludwig yelled through the door. "I've got company."

By dinner, I was too wasted to speak. Stephen and Ludwig guffawed into the night, reliving their college pranks. I retreated to the den and curled up on the couch.

Saturday morning, we followed Ludwig in his pick-up truck to the takeout on the Lost. The road paralleled the river, which lay out of sight on the far side of the valley just beneath the brow of a wooded ridge. The highway wound up a hill. Ludwig pulled onto the shoulder and motioned for me to park.

"Takeout's down this path. Leave your car here and put your canoe in the pick-up."

I peered through the leafless trees, eager to see where the river disappeared into the mountain. I asked Ludwig if he'd ever seen this famous spot.

"Heard about it, never seen it. For all I know, the guys who named this river were high on somethin'. They probably paddled upstream by mistake, and when the river petered out, they made up some bullshit about it disappearing into a mountain. Fuckin' hillbillies."

We stopped laughing when we reach the put-in. The Lost was so shallow it looked to be paved in cobblestones. I asked about putting in farther downstream, but Ludwig knew of no other access.

"Hell, it's only five miles to the takeout. Worse comes to worse, you can walk the damn thing."

Stephen and I bid Ludwig farewell. We turned and faced the river.

"Why don't you take the stern," Stephen asked. "You're the one that knows how to paddle."

"I'll call out the rocks," I said.

"Fine."

It had been years since I'd paddled this small canoe tandem. Stephen had to cram himself into the bow, his knees rising high over the gunwales. I had to turn my boots at an angle to fit them under the stern seat.

We pushed off the bank and paddled to mid-stream, prying off the bottom all the way. Fifty yards along, we ran aground.

"Backpaddle," I said.

We pushed against the bottom.

"Jerk it."

The boat wouldn't move.

"You need to get out, Stephen."

He stepped into the ankle-deep water and lifted the bow off the rock. We paddled another ten yards and ran aground.

"Backwater. Jerk it."

Stephen slumped over his paddle. "Why do *I* need to get out?"

"Because the bow is on a rock; that's why."

Stephen yanked the boat sideways. We paddled on.

"Draw left," I said. "Left!"

The canoe screeched to a halt. Stephen slammed his paddle down. "Will you quit yelling?"

"I'm not yelling."

"You're ruining the whole fucking mood."

"Fine. I'll *speak* the orders instead of shouting them."

A rock loomed ahead. I composed myself as best I could. "Go left," I said in an even voice.

Too late. We banged against the rock and yawed perilously to one side.

"This is *not* going to work, Stephen."

"All right, try this. I'll point which way we should go, and you turn the boat in that direction."

"What?"

"I point. You turn."

"Every time you point, you'll have to let go of your paddle."

"Let's. Just. Try it."

The current picked up speed, the rocks came on fast. Stephen pointed to the left, took two strokes, pointed to the right. We hit and swung halfway around, coming aground sideways to the current.

"This is bullshit," I said.

"All right, let's just try paddling without talking."

"You mean *feel* our way through? This is not a Zen archery course, Stephen. This is a fucking river. I know how to get down these things."

I couldn't believe this was happening. We'd had such high hopes for this day—the wild boys cruising down a river, hawks circling overhead. Maybe this hole in the mountain would make up for it.

We paddled on, banging against rocks. As the river grew deeper, I stole glances at the wooded hillsides. The dogwoods were budding out. In another week, everything would be in bloom.

We came upon a grassy cove at the head of a narrow gorge. An old log cabin—the remains of one—stood in the middle of a wheat-colored meadow. We pulled ashore and circled the ruin. The log walls had collapsed. Through a warped window frame, I glimpsed rusted mattress springs and tattered newspaper. Someone had planted daffodils around the foundation. I thought of the hopes they must have had for their little home. What had happened to cause them to leave this corner of paradise?

"You wanna eat?" Stephen asked.

"Yeah, sure."

"I'll get the cooler."

We sat on a log and ate our sandwiches in silence. Stephen announced he was going for a walk. I lay back amidst the daffodils and closed my eyes. The light came and went as clouds passed before the sun. I stretched my arm across my faced, rolled onto my side. The sun disappeared and I looked up to see an enormous black cloud welling over the ridge. There came a flash of lightening followed by a clap of thunder. Stephen came running across the meadow.

"Man the boats!" he shouted.

We launched into the river, hoping to outrun the storm. A sound like gravel being poured from a dump truck closed from behind, and I turned to see the surface of the river popping like hot grease in a frying pan. The raindrops hit with the force of BBs. We hunched our shoulders and fled into the gorge—no choice now but to paddle on. With every flash of lightning, the rock walls leapt forth in bold relief. Shock waves of thunder echoed through the canyon. With our knees planted on the wet aluminum hull, we were the perfect lighting rod. We could die at any moment.

In the midst of the storm, I realized we were zooming untouched down the rapids. We slid down chutes and bounced through tail waves.

"Hey, Stephen, we're doing good!"

"Yeah, too bad we gotta die!"

All too soon, the current slowed. The rain subsided, and the flashes grew faint. The sun broke through the clouds. Glancing at the hillside, I caught the reflection of a car window.

"There's our car," I said. "We must be getting close."

I rose up on my knees and scanned the river ahead. Would there be a dark hole like the mouth of a cave? A giant whirlpool?

The ridgeline loomed close. Giant boulders clogged the narrow channel, the remnants of some ancient landslide. I slowed the canoe, cruised the edge of the rock pile. The river did, in fact, disappear, but the cleft in the ridge left no secret as to where it went.

"This is it?" Stephen asked.

"Guess so."

"I thought the guy said it disappeared into the side of a mountain."

"That's what he said."

"The lyin' bag of shit."

We circled once around the muddy pool; then hauled the canoe out onto the bank. Stephen sat down and rolled a joint. I turned the canoe over. Dozens of new scratches marred the hull. One of the aluminum ribs had popped loose.

"This doesn't look too good," I said.

"Ah, fuck it."

Stephen lit the joint and passed it over. I took a long hit, grew dizzy but not high. Tandem canoeing has a way revealing essential truths about relationships. Two people bound together, same goal, different responsibilities. How you react when things get tough says a lot about your ability to live together. Stephen and I had not done well for awhile. And I had a new opportunity.

I passed the joint. "Remember Mr. Talbott?"

"Bud Talbott? Lives in Cleveland?"

"Yeah. He's a friend of my Dad's. He's started something called the Ohio Conservation Foundation, promoting the environment. He wants me to work for him."

"He just called you out of the blue?"

"No. I was talking to him when I was home over Christmas. I told him about that bill to create a Cuyahoga National Recreation Area. I said I could help promote it."

"Back in Cleveland?"

"Yes."

Stephen exhaled and lay back in the grass. This was big for us. We had both moved here with such high hopes. To change the world. To break away from the past. And we truly did love each other. But we could not live together.

"Well," Stephen said. "You'll probably be good at it."

Chapter 4
The Cuyahoga

The Manuel men have a long history with the Cuyahoga River, at least the part that flows through the City of Cleveland. For forty years, the *John S. Manuel*, a 500-foot-long steamship named after my grandfather, wound its way up the Cuyahoga from Lake Erie to deliver iron ore to the steel mills. My Uncle David Manuel owned a tanker, the *Marine Fuel Oil*, that plied the same stretch of river, refueling the ore carriers before their return trip to the mines. Dad's office on the twenty-second floor of the Illuminating Co. Building looked down on the mouth of the Cuyahoga, its dirty brown tongue protruding into the ashen gray of the dying lake.

The summer after my junior year in high school, I worked on the Cuyahoga as first mate on the *Marine Fuel Oil*. When not fueling an ore carrier, the ship was tied to a rusting bulkhead in an area known as the Flats—a serpentine floodplain covered with railyards, refineries, and steel mills. Day and night, smoke billowed from the fat stacks of the mills and blue flames from the thinner stacks of the refineries. The sky was hazy white, and the air reeked of petrochemicals and asphalt.

For most of the day, I worked alone, pushing a three-inch-wide scraper across the hot steel deck to prepare the tanker for a new coat of paint. A stone's throw away on the other side of the river, hammer mills banged inside the windowless expanse of the Republic Steel Mill. Particles rained down from the smoke stacks, coating the deck, my car, and my back with fine red dust.

At least once a day, a deep blast from an air horn jerked me upright, and I turned to see a tugboat straining to pull a freighter around the bend. The siren sounded on the Jefferson Street Bridge, and the trestle rose until one end pointed straight up in the air. Yard by yard, the ore boat came into view, tall as a grain silo, longer than a football field. If the ship needed refueling, Captain Stan and Co-captain Eddie arrived from their homes in the West Side. I put away the paint scraper and cast off the heavy, oiled ropes. Stan fired up the twin diesels, and we headed upriver to where the ore boat was docked.

I loved cruising the Cuyahoga on the *Marine Fuel Oil*, moving like a king through the heart of the city. I leaned against the rail in jeans and a t-shirt, nodding at the mill workers who came out to eat lunch at the water's edge. Office towers commanded the high ground, but I didn't envy the lawyers and accountants stuck behind desks in their starched white shirts. I was a working man.

And the river? The Cuyahoga was a sacrificial lamb to this great industrial enterprise. Raw sewage from the boats, process water from the mills, spilled oil and iron ore pellets—all of it went straight into the river. Biologists said the lower Cuyahoga was devoid of life, caustic enough to peel the paint from a ship's hull. It sure didn't have much of a current. I remembered seeing piles of oil-soaked debris float past the tanker one day and, driven by an onshore wind, drift back upstream the next.

Then, in the summer of 1969, the Cuyahoga caught fire. A spark from a welder's torch drifted down from a bridge and ignited the oil-soaked surface. At first, no one thought to call the fire department. Oil patches had burned on the river before to no great effect. Then, the fire spread to the shipyards of the Great Lakes Towing Company and the Jefferson Street Bridge. The Cleveland Fire Department arrived and blasted the river with its hoses, fighting water with water.

Reading about it in the morning paper, seeing the picture of that clean, white water arcing toward the tower of flame, I simply laughed. The river was already dead. This was just its cremation. But others had seen enough. In the coming years, the fire on the Cuyahoga became the rallying point for a growing army of people who believed that things could change, that the rivers could be saved. Books were written. Rallies were staged. Laws were passed. And across the country, non-profit organizations were formed to push this new environmental agenda. One of those was the Ohio Conservation Foundation.

* * *

"I can't believe you voted for Nixon, Dad. He's such a crook."

Seated at the dining table of my parent's house, my younger sister, Annie, flipped through the *Cleveland Plain Dealer*, scoffing at the latest news about Watergate. She was never one to hide her opinions, but being the youngest, she was spared the brunt of Dad's anger.

Dad shoved his scrambled eggs around his plate. "I suppose I should have voted for McGovern like Johnny did," he said. "Then we could nationalize the steel industry."

"Oh, darling, don't exaggerate," Mom said. "You know he hasn't proposed that."

Brother Peter sat next to me in his white cotton "pajamas," a souvenir from his semester in India studying the sitar. He spat a half-chewed mouthful of eggs onto his plate and poked around with his finger. "Out, out, damn shell," he said, raising his finger aloft.

Dad rolled his eyes. "When do you start work, Johnny?" he said.

"Monday."

"How about your apartment?"

"I'm moving in tomorrow."

Dad nodded. "I suppose you could ride the rapid transit with me."

I was moving to an apartment in Cleveland Heights specifically to be out from under my father's glare.

"No, Dad. We're on different lines."

Each morning in that apartment, I put on my coat and tie and rode the Blue Line to work. I emerged from the station beneath Terminal Tower, crossed Public Square, and headed up Euclid Avenue to the Arcade, a once-fashionable shopping center built in the Gilded Age, but now housing a tired collection of wig shops and offices.

Mike McDermitt—Big Mike—served as director of the Ohio Conservation Foundation. A former college basketball star turned king of the Cleveland slow-pitch softball league, Mike was nominally committed to saving the environment, but more at home gladhanding state legislators and Chamber of Commerce types. That suited me fine; we needed their support to advance our agenda of promoting clean rivers and open space. And it let me focus on my strength—writing.

"Hey, Shakespeare," Mike called from his next door office, "I've got to give a speech to the Rotary Club. Write me some of that purple prose. But nothing about that woodpecker."

"Pileated?"

"Yeah, that one."

Aside from speech writing, my duties revolved around building support for the proposed Cuyahoga Valley National Park, the bill for which awaited action by Congress. I had sold Bud Talbott, Director of the Foundation Board, on the idea that the park could become a reality if it gained popular support.

Selling a Cuyahoga Valley National Park wasn't easy. Most people laughed at the mention of the name. "Isn't that the river that caught on fire?" I didn't hold out much hope for resurrecting the portion that ran through the Flats. But upstream of Cleveland, the river flowed through a wooded floodplain paralleled by the old Ohio and Erie Canal and bisected by hemlock-shaded ravines. America was in the midst of the fuel crisis, and the federal government was keen on developing recreation areas near major population centers. For millions of people in northern Ohio, the Cuyahoga Valley could offer a place to ride bikes along the towpath or to hike beside a hissing waterfall.

In magazine articles, speeches, and slide shows, I waxed eloquent about the white-tailed deer and the red-tailed hawks, the historic Hale Farm and Brandywine Falls. I avoided mentioning the river itself. I'd glimpsed the upper reaches of the Cuyahoga from several bridge crossings. It didn't look half-bad, but water quality officials warned that looks were deceiving.

The major problem, they explained, was that the City of Akron's sewage treatment plant emptied into the Cuyahoga just upstream from the proposed park. Via a Combined Sewer Outlet (CSO), the plant processed both wastewater from homes and businesses and stormwater that ran off city streets and parking lots. In dry weather the plant could handle both loads, but after heavy rains, it was overwhelmed. Raw sewage flowed straight into the river and could leave the water toxic for weeks thereafter.

I asked a water quality official if there were times when the river was safe to run.

"Probably," he said. "There's just no way of knowing in any immediate fashion. Water samples take weeks to analyze, and by the time you get the results, the conditions may have changed."

Meanwhile, Dad and I continued our old dance. I came home on weekends to see friends and enjoy some free meals. Dad would pour me a martini, and we'd sit in the sunporch overlooking the Chagrin. He asked about work. I described my latest press release. Then, he floated the idea of my looking for a "real" job.

"Stuey Harrison says he's got something in the accounting department at Cleveland Cliffs. Why don't you give him a call?"

"Dad, I've *got* a job!"

Come spring, we closed the office early on Fridays. Mike had softball practice at five, and I got into a pick-up game with some friends in Hunting Valley. I was crossing Public Square one Friday afternoon headed for the rapid transit when I saw Dad coming the other way. What the hell was he doing here?

I tried to blend in with the crowd, but he sniffed me out and blocked my path. "Where do you think you're going?"

"Home."

"Home? It's 4:30."

"Dad, it's Friday."

While a crowd of office workers streamed past, he lectured me on the value of working an eight-hour day. He swiped his hand across my long hair and jabbed at the stains on my necktie. The old rage welled up inside of me. One more insult and I was out of there.

Later that month, Mike appeared at my desk wearing an impish smile. "You're in luck, Shakespeare. The Sierra Club is sponsoring a canoe trip down the upper Cuyahoga. I think I've got a game that weekend."

He handed me the invitation and snickered. "Bring me back some of that granola stuff."

The morning of the trip, I packed my camera gear and headed south of Cleveland on Interstate 271. The clouds were breaking up after an all-night rain, the air full of springtime smells. Where the interstate crossed over the valley, I stared out at a landscape colored pastel green and pink. The exit took me on a two-lane that descended to the valley floor. I pulled over behind a group of cars with canoe racks.

"Hey, you must be the guy from the Foundation."

A tall, red-headed man approached with an outstretched hand. "Ron Kovacs, president of the local chapter."

Two heavy-set boys wearing lumber jackets and nervous smiles stood at a distance. "That's J.P. and Larry. They're both new members." And experienced canoeists, no doubt. Larry looked especially convincing in his Australian digger hat.

"Over here we've got Vic and Dennis..."

Vic and Dennis offered quick waves and returned to packing their canoe. Behind them, the Cuyahoga ran like a giant conveyor belt, cocoa brown, aswirl with rips and boils.

I sniffed the air. "Smells like sewage."

Ron sighed. "We got a good drenching last night. That darned treatment plant must've overflowed."

"And what is that all over the bushes?"

All along the bank, the branches near the waterline were covered with wet toilet paper. I walked to the bank, felt a chill rising off the water.

"Are you sure we should be running this?" I asked.

"Heck, yes, it's gonna be a beautiful day."

Ron read out the boat assignments: "J.P. and Larry, you're in the yellow canoe. Vic and Dennis in the red. John, you don't mind paddling bow, do you?"

Oh, great. The bow. I'd gotten comfortable paddling up front in my Keewaydin days, but when you don't know the stern paddler, the bow can be unnerving. You can't see what the sternman is doing, and it's hard to correct for mistakes.

"Fellas, John and I are going to be running sweep. I've got a whistle, so if anybody gets in trouble, I'll give three quick blasts. That means stop. Immediately!"

I knelt down in the front seat. The boat wobbled as Ron stepped in the stern. Every muscle in my body tensed.

"Let's paddle out and wait for the others," Ron said.

We pushed off the bank and paddled to midstream. I drew on the left to get the bow headed into the current. As the stern fishtailed into line, a frantic yelp rose from behind. I turned to see Ron fallen backward on the seat, feet in the air. He pulled himself up, face gone white. Now, I was scared. Capsize in this filth, and you were bound to get sick. I glanced at the bank. There was still time to back out. Then, Vic and Dennis flashed by in their yellow canoe. J.P. and Larry followed, gripping their paddles by the shafts. Ron yelled after them, "Hold your paddles by the handles. By the handles!"

We turned and followed, swept along in the fast-moving current. I squatted down on my haunches. I didn't want this canoe going anywhere but straight ahead.

As we raced down the river, I couldn't help staring at the banks. Every branch was snagged with refuse—toilet paper, tampons, condoms. I laughed. "We should declare this a Wild and Septic River."

"What?"

Around every other bend, a tree lay fallen in the river. "Strainers" are a canoeist's worst nightmare, often lying right in the path of the main current. Water will flow around a rock, but it goes under and through the branches of a tree. If you hit a strainer in a canoe, you'll be turned sideways and flipped. You may get washed downstream, or you may get snagged by a branch, in which case you're in for trouble.

As each strainer came into sight, Dennis shouted a warning. Ron and I charged for the opposite side of the river, but J.P. and Larry were slow to react, clearing the outstretched branches by the slimmest of margins.

"How far to Peninsula?" I asked.

"Should be coming up shortly."

Peninsula is an historic riverside town that park supporters billed as a sure-fire attraction. This was where people would come to rent bikes and shop for antiques. A scenic railroad running up the valley from Cleveland would stop here.

A low bridge appeared, marking the approach into town. I caught a glimpse of the rooflines bordering Main Street and the train-station-turned-café. We could be in there now having coffee.

A cordon of trees closed off the view. Up ahead, the interstate towered over the river on giant cement pillars. That hemlock-shaded ledge should be around here somewhere. I took out my camera and searched the horizon. There were the trees, but where was the ledge? The river swirled on silent and menacing.

North of the interstate, the Cuyahoga meandered through a wide floodplain. Head-high banks blocked the view of the surrounding farmland. I felt as if we're paddling through a drainage ditch.

"Strainer!"

Vic and Dennis darted toward midstream. The tree appeared at the inside of the bend. J.P. and Larry angled away, but the current was too strong. Branches crackled as the canoe broached sideways. Both paddlers disappeared.

Ron blew his whistle: "Boat over!"

We flew past the tree as the boat rolled under. A long second passed before Larry surfaced downstream, water streaming out of the pinned-up side of his hat. The canoe bobbed up behind us, J.P. holding onto the stern.

Ron shouted to Vic, "Grab the canoe. We'll get Larry."

The current swept Larry to the outside of the bend and along the sheer mud wall. He clawed at the bank like a cockroach in a toilet bowl. Each time he gained a handhold, the dirt gave way, and he slipped beneath the surface.

I spotted some bushes hanging just above the river. "Up there. Let's pin him against the bank," I shouted.

We angled toward shore. Larry grabbed the gunwales; Ron reached for a branch. As the canoe jerked to a halt, I hoisted myself onto the bank. Behind me, the bushes crackled to life. A furry brown shape dove into the narrow gap between the canoe and the bank. Two more followed, each disappearing into the water before I could tell what they are. A fourth hit the gunwale and tumbled at Ron's feet in the canoe. A baby beaver!

"Get him out," Ron said.

I let go of Larry and reached for the beaver. He clicked his front teeth. I pulled my hand away.

"Get the beaver out!"

I reached for the hard, stubby tail and lifted the animal in the air. "Who'd ever think something like this could live in the Cuyahoga?" I said.

"Get rid of him! And help Larry, for Chris' sakes."

I'd forgotten about Larry, clinging to the gunwales. I tossed the beaver in the river and grabbed Larry by the collar.

"Can you make it up?"

Larry shook his head. I mustered all my strength, leaned back and hauled him onto the bank.

"How ya' doin', man?" I said. "You gonna make it?"

He stared at me from beneath his jaunty hat, leaned over and barfed in the grass.

Chapter 5
The Upper Haw

The interstate ran due south from Cleveland to Bluefield, West Virginia. There it reverted to a two-lane highway that zigzagged up the blue-green wall of the Appalachian Mountains. At each turn, the horizon fell farther below. I crested the ridge and left the past behind.

The road hugged the contours of the land, dipping and rising through tawny meadows and forests of white pine. Holsteins stood watch on the steep hillsides. Down in the valleys, sunlight glinted off rushing streams.

I nudged the Capri toward the guardrail, hoping for a better view. Dark water tumbled between banks of rhododendron and mountain laurel. At each stream crossing, I recited the names on the little green signs—Big Reed Island Creek, Clear Creek, Laurel Fork. I wanted to explore every one.

Just past the town of Max Meadows, the road ran onto a long steel-truss bridge. The New River fanned out shallow, wide, and clear from between the low green hills, tumbling at intervals over broad ledges. Lights flashed in the distance—the reflection of sunlight off moving paddles. Canoeists.

I slowed for a better look, until a pick-up truck beeped behind me. I didn't know how far this river was from my ultimate destination, Chapel Hill, North Carolina, but I was coming back.

I left the river and drove on through the ridgetop towns of Hillsville and Fancy Gap, a marine blue sky above. Just past the North Carolina state line, the highway began to drop. Switchbacks that had lifted me up only hours before pulled me down out of the mountains and into the hazy piedmont. The landscape lost its edge. The air grew hot and humid. By the time I reached Chapel Hill, I was thoroughly depressed.

The University of North Carolina stood atop a hill within a neighborhood of Victorian homes. Behind a statue of a Confederate soldier, students strolled along brick paths under the shade of massive poplar and oaks. As I pulled up to the light at Franklin and Henderson, three women stepped off the curb wearing flip-flops and cut-off jeans. I opened my window and breathed the heavy air tinged with the scent of magnolia.

I spotted her from behind, riding a ten-speed bike against the flow of traffic. Her long, white legs easily worked the pedals, blonde curls tumbling onto broad shoulders. She glanced over but didn't see me, her wide cheekbones tapering to a half-smile. "I'm gonna meet that one," I said.

I drove the length of Franklin Street and entered the town of Carrboro, then Chapel Hill's blue-collar neighbor. The apartment stood at the end of a graveled street, two-story brick, no landscaping. The manager flicked on the overhead light to reveal a linoleum tile floor, wicker furniture, plywood cabinets. A piece of shit, but it would do. I put my clothes in the bureau, shoes in the closet. I lay down on the bed, stared at the sprayed-on ceiling, and started to cry.

My reason for coming to Chapel Hill was to attend UNC's School of City and Regional Planning. I wanted to learn how to clean up rivers, to administer the new laws that banned industry from dumping their crap in the water, to design sewage treatment systems that wouldn't overflow, to plant fields so the soil didn't run off every time it rained.

And I wanted to start a new life, away from my parents, from the n'er do wells who hung around Gates Mills waiting for the motivation to step into their father's shoes. I wanted to expose myself, to what I wasn't sure. Something deeper. A new river.

Classes at the School of City and Regional Planning didn't start for a week. I wandered the streets alone, looking in store windows, sitting on stone walls. The woman with the blonde curls was nowhere to be seen.

I stopped into a bar, thinking the gaiety of a crowd would lift my spirits. But their laughter only magnified my isolation. Everyone seemed to know each other. They spoke a language I didn't understand:

"Carver's here with Missy."

"Ah naay!"

"I got me a new truck."

"Ass grite!"

Walking back to my apartment, I came upon a narrow building with a promising sign—Haw River Paddle Shop. I peered through the window at a dark shape that hung from the ceiling—a canoe. It wasn't aluminum or wood-and-canvas. It was made of something else. I'd be back to check this out.

The door stood open the following morning. The proprietor nodded as I stepped inside, dark eyes watching through an orb of curly black hair and beard. I glanced at the knives in the display case, the paddles on the wall. The canoe hung from the ceiling, forest green, just like the ones at Keewaydin. I ran my fingers along the hull. "What's this made of?"

"ABS," the man said. "Vinyl on the outside and foam in the middle. Slides over rocks like you won't believe."

I walked around the bow. "How much does it weigh?"

"About eighty pounds. More than aluminum, but a lot less than wood and canvas."

The man came out from behind the counter. "You aren't from around here, are you?"

"Nope. Ohio."

"Is your name John Manuel?"

I turned and stared.

"Jim East. I was in your brother's class in high school."

It took me a minute to recognize the face behind the mass of hair. "East! My God! What are you doing down here?"

"To be near my dad. He split up with my mom, and he's living over in Durham."

I laughed. "I came down here to get *away* from my dad."

We talked of goings-on in Cleveland, my brother's latest excursion to India, sister Susie's work as a rafting guide in California. I turned back to the canoe.

"Are there any rivers down here? I didn't see anything after I left the mountains."

"There's a nice one south of town called the Haw."

"Any rapids?"

"Hell, yes. The Upper Haw's mostly Class Is and IIs. The Lower Haw's got IIs and IIIs. It's pretty low right now, but wait 'till spring."

I confessed that I wasn't up on this new river terminology.

"Class I is basically a riffle or a little ledge like that one below the dam at Gates Mills—anything you can run straight on. Class II rapids require a little maneuvering, but won't hurt you if you fuck up. Think a series of foot-high standing waves or a wide S-turn around a couple of rocks. Class IIIs are like big drops with a keeper hole or a twisty passage where you can pin a boat if you fall off your line."

I examined the price tag on the boat. "$850! I guess I'll be renting."

"I've got lots of rentals. But you really ought to have your own boat. I've got some factory seconds coming in next month. They came out of the mold with soft noses, but you can patch 'em up with a fiberglass kit. I'll sell you one for five hundred dollars."

My boat arrived in mid-September—a 16-foot Mad River Explorer, fire-engine red with blond wood gunwales and cane seats. I built a roof rack out of two-by-fours and gutter mounts and drove the canoe back to my apartment.

Several days passed before I could screw up the courage to patch the nose. The materials were new to me: fiberglass cloth and epoxy glue in two parts, a clear resin and a hardener. Once you mixed them together, there was no turning back.

I laid the cloth against the bow and brushed on the epoxy. Jim said it was important to put down enough layers to protect the bow from hard knocks, but not so much that it won't cut through the water.

I let the epoxy dry overnight and put on a second layer. Next morning, I drove the boat down to University Lake and set it in the water. The trim looked good from front to back. The cane seat crackled as I eased myself down. I took a few forward strokes and let her glide. Nice and straight. I had myself a boat.

As summer turned to fall, the humidity vanished, and the campus oaks glowed like burnished copper. The sun shone day after day, something that never happened in Cleveland. I made several friends among classmates, and together we explored the clubs on Franklin Street, the house parties on McCauley, and football games in Kenan Stadium.

Over Christmas break, I returned to Cleveland. Dad was mollified that I was back in school, though he was baffled why I had chosen the South.

"Trying to be a big fish in a small pond?" he asked.

"They actually have good schools there, Dad. People come from all over the country."

"Do they have a Yale Club?"

In January, I vacated my apartment and moved into a house with two friends. It wasn't much to look at—a faded maroon bungalow covered with board-and-batten siding. But the hardwood floors felt good underfoot, and the big double-hung windows let in the morning sun. I bought a queen-sized mattress that covered half the bedroom floor. I needed a woman to share it.

A classmate invited me to a party at her house in the country. She said she lived with two other women in an old farmhouse. They cooked and heated with a wood-burning stove and drew their water from a well. This I had to see.

I followed Old 86 through the moonlit countryside to the north end of the county. The rutted driveway ran on forever between stubblefields of corn. I parked next to a line of Toyotas and Volvos with mud-spattered doors.

The farmhouse stood beneath a pair of giant oaks, windows aglow like a ship at sea. I strode toward the front porch and fell flat on my face, my pant leg sporting a new tear. What kind of idiot would string a barbed wire fence around his house? I knocked on the door, and the bicycling woman with the blonde curls answered.

"Sorry about the fence," Cathy said. "We put it up to keep the cows away from the daffodils."

She was as pretty as I'd remembered—wide cheekbones, green eyes, thin lips slightly parted, as if she, too, recognized me from somewhere. She led me inside where a crowd of strangers dressed in jeans and hiking boots packed the small rooms. My friend, Pat, was making hash brownies in the kitchen. I said a quick hello, then slipped back through the crowd. Cathy was standing alone in the corner.

"What is it you do, again?" I said.

"Instructional design."

She launched into an explanation. I didn't hear a word. I was dazzled by her eyes, the way she kept them focused on me. She didn't have a boyfriend.

Over the coming weeks, we made excuses to see each other. I went out to chop wood. She came in to use my shower. The third time she visited, I waited in the bedroom. She emerged in a towel, carrying her change of clothes.

"Why don't you leave those off?" I said.

Over the next three months, we burned up the pavement on Highway 86, driving the twenty miles back and forth every few days. It would have been easier to move in together, but we were cautious people. She wasn't sure if I was interested in a long-term relationship. I wasn't sure how she'd be in a canoe.

Come the first of May, I popped the question. "Would you like to go canoeing?" I asked.

"I'd love to go," she said. "But I've never done whitewater."

"I'll show you."

Jim East said the upper Haw was the best place to take a novice paddler, and he agreed to be our guide. We met him at the canoe shop and followed his battered pick-up truck south into Chatham County. For an Ohio boy, the Chatham landscape had the closed-in feel of the tropics. Kudzu vines hung like shrouds over the trees. Water seeped from the red clay banks.

When we rode out onto Chicken Bridge, I brightened. "There's the Haw," I said to Cathy.

The river stretched dark and lovely between the arching boughs of sycamores. It was the first place I'd been in the area where you could see the clouds on the horizon. We parked beside the wooden bridge and carried the boats down to the water. I held the gunwale while Cathy settled in the bow.

"How's it feel up there?" I said.

"Good."

We pushed off the bank and fell in behind Jim. I could see that Cathy had a good stroke. She gripped the paddle with one hand atop the handle and the other at the bottom of the shaft. Her movements were strong, but unhurried.

"Try leaning forward when you place the paddle; then draw yourself upright," I said. "That way, you use your back muscles instead of your arms."

She nodded, adjusted her motion.

As we rounded the bend, the current picked up speed, spidery boils rising from the depths.

"Those swirls are nothing to worry about, just some kind of underwater turbulence," I said. "But if you see a stationary V like that one, there's a stick or a rock right beneath the surface. Stay away from those."

I liked that Cathy didn't feel the need to talk. She scanned the banks with a serene smile, followed a crow as it flew across the channel.

"Sawtooth Ledge coming up," Jim said. "Stay to the left."

Cathy shipped her paddle. "O.K., John, tell me what to do."

I asked her to show me a draw stroke. She pivoted to the right, planted her paddle in the water, and drew the blade toward the hull.

"That's good. Now, reach way out."

She took three powerful strokes, pulling the bow across the water.

"Perfect. That's all you'll need for now."

Jim hugged the inside of the bend, riding the deep water that ran along the bank. We ducked beneath sycamore branches popping in and out of the sunlight.

"Keep us against the bank," I said.

A broken line of white "roostertails" marked where the ledge angled in from river right.

"Get ready with that draw," I said. "When we come to the ledge, look for a V facing upstream. That'll be the deepest water."

Jim darted into midstream to avoid a cluster of rocks.

"Now!"

Cathy leaned out and dug her paddle in deep. We broke into sunlight and bore down on the ledge. Cathy lined the bow up perfectly. A few quick strokes in the stern, and we slid right down the V.

Jim waited in an eddy at the bottom of the rapid, watching us with furrowed brow. As we flew past, Cathy swatted the water with her paddle and sprayed Jim right in the face.

I grinned at Jim as if I were in on the plot, but this girl took us both by surprise.

Below Sawtooth, the river slowed. I settled into the rhythm of camp days, long strokes and steady breathing. I scanned the banks for wildlife. Atop an overhanging branch, I found what I was looking for.

"Snake," I said. "Let's check it out."

I turned the boat toward shore, drifting to a halt a paddle length away from the branch. Bullet-headed and heavy-bodied, the water snake stretched out for at least a yard.

Cathy leaned away. "I don't like snakes, John."

"It's a banded water snake. Not poisonous."

"I don't care. We had water moccasins in Florida. They weren't something you fooled with."

I took a stroke forward, moved Cathy away and me within arm's reach. The snake was on the verge of molting, his eyes covered by a milky sheen. I waved my hand in front of his face. His yellow tongue flicked the air.

"He knows something's near," I said. "He can sense the heat."

"Why doesn't he move?"

"He's half-blind, for one. And his senses are probably a little dulled after a long winter. Takes 'em awhile to warm up."

"Let's go."

We paddled around the bend where the river meandered through a wide boulder garden. Jim picked out a flat rock in midstream and declared a lunch break. I sat down on my life jacket and stretched my bare legs out on the warm rock.

"Beer?" Jim said.

I hesitated. Didn't we need to be on our toes?

"Relax, man," Jim said. "This is the upper Haw."

Across the wide channel, the rippling water parted around big gray rocks of Carolina slate. The Haw had sculpted them into scalloped curves, her own reclining nudes. One held a neat pile of tiny clam shells, the leavings of an otter.

I studied the tall stand of loblolly pines on the far shore. A white spot stood out against the dark green of the needles. Suddenly, it sprouted wings and soared out across the river.

I shouted, "That's an eagle. A bald eagle!"

All my life, I'd wanted to see one of these birds. Growing up in the 1950s and 60s, I was convinced it would never happen. Eagles were destined for extinction, their eggshells rendered overly fragile by the pesticide DDT. That chemical was sprayed across the land, where it ran into streams and ingested by fish, the eagles prey. Laws had been passed to ban DDT, but the results were slow in coming. But here was proof that things could change.

The eagle swooped down, yellow talons raking the surface. I marveled as he rose with a fish. "He got one!"

As the eagle flew downstream, I threw my hands atop my head. Cathy beamed.

Jim sipped the last of his beer. "You guys ready to roll?"

We packed up the canoes and headed back on the river. The temperature had climbed into the eighties. Cathy took half a dozen strokes, then laid her paddle across the gunwales. She took off her lifejacket, crossed her arms and lifted her T-shirt over her head. She wasn't wearing a bra.

The sight of her breasts, just the outermost curve, lit me on fire. She refastened her life jacket and picked up her paddle.

"O.K., I'm ready."

As we worked our way through the boulder garden, the current picked up speed. Tongues of whitewater lapped at the red hull.

"Here we go." I leaned into my stroke, drove the canoe toward the openings in the rocks. The rush of water filled the air, the shoreline blurred. "Keep paddling!"

The rapids came one after another—Beginner's Peril, Little Nantahala, Final Solution. We moved in perfect harmony, switching sides, shouting, delirious.

We rode the tail wave, exhausted but wanting more. The current slowed and widened as the river backed up behind the

Bynum dam. As we made our way toward the takeout, the smell of honeysuckle wafted out from the banks. A bare spot marked the finish. We hauled the canoe onto the ground and laid the paddles in the hull.

Cathy beamed. "That was fun!"

"Really? You liked it?"

I was momentarily confused by her approach. Then she took my head in her hands and parted my lips with her tongue.

Chapter 6
The Lower Haw

The rain fell hard all night. In the morning, I dialed the Haw River Paddle Shop. "What's the river at, Jim?"

"A foot-and-a-half."

"Wow, that's high!"

"You guys can handle it. We're meeting at the dam at eleven."

I covered the receiver and turned to Cathy. "It's at a foot-and-a-half."

"That's higher than we've ever done it."

"Jim says we'll be all right."

"Okay."

I loved this about Cathy—her physical bravery, her trust in me as a paddler. In the two years we'd been canoeing together, we'd become a good team. We'd run the Nantahala River in the North Carolina mountains and the Chattooga River in Georgia. We'd graduated from the Upper to the Lower Haw.

The Lower Haw was a different animal from the Upper, with many more rapids and trickier ones at that. Local river rats boasted about its rapids like parents do of their smarter child's grades.

As with any river, the difficulty of the Haw varies with the volume and speed of the water. Rapids that provide a nice bounce at low levels morph into monster waves at high levels.

Every few years, some fools tried to run the Lower Haw at flood stage and ended up drowning or clinging to a rock from which they needed to be rescued by helicopter.

Water levels on the Haw and most other rivers are now continuously recorded by U.S. Geological Survey monitoring stations and posted on the Web. But for years, the only way to know the water level on the Haw was to drive down to Bynum and check the hand-painted gauge on the southern most pylon of the Bynum Road bridge. A reading of "0" was the minimum you could run without scraping bottom. Six inches was a good level, enough to carry you over the rocks but not to create any killer waves. At a foot-and-a-half above "0," the Haw edged into dangerous territory. Make a mistake at this level, and the river would not forgive.

I loaded the canoe on the Capri while Cathy made sandwiches. Sydney, our black lab, ran circles around the car, hoping to be included on the trip. Syd was our surrogate child, a way to test our ability to care for something or someone aside from ourselves. We'd managed pretty well as a threesome, and after living together for two years, Cathy and I decided to marry.

Then, almost as soon as we made the announcement, I got cold feet. Cathy went to Africa on a month-long work trip during which I imagined that long, winding river. It was impossible to know what rapids we might encounter or what skills it might take to run them. Any guide will tell you that's a river you shouldn't run.

"Baby, I've been thinking ..." I said the night she returned.

She stared at me across the pillow. "I've been thinking, too."

"I don't want to call the whole thing off, but let's give it some more time."

She agreed. I prayed that somehow the right decision would eventually bubble up from the depths.

* * *

We pulled off the highway into the rutted gravel parking lot just below the Bynum dam. The lot was jammed with mud-spattered vehicles bearing an assortment of homemade roof racks. Jim was standing next to two other guys, each with his own boat, kayaks. Jim had "gone to the dark side" as we canoeists used to say. I couldn't blame him. Kayaks were more maneuverable than canoes, and if you flipped, you could roll them upright. But they only carried one person, and I knew that if I were to switch to a kayak, Cathy would stop paddling. And she and I were in this together.

I had done my best to make our Explorer more suited to whitewater. I'd glued thigh straps in the bow and stern that allowed you to lean out to the side while keeping your weight low in the boat. I'd installed air bags in the bow, stern, and center that deflected water and kept the boat floating high if you flipped. But you still had to muster your own courage.

We carried our boats down to the put-in below the dam. Water was pouring over in a thundering sheet, filling the air with a chugging sound like a subterranean steam engine.

"Watch yourself today," Jim said. "River's got a lot of push."

We set our boats in the water and paddled along the foam line below the dam to get clear of the near shore rocks. Then we turned and raced past the dark pylons of the old Bynum Bridge beyond.

Jim glanced at the gauge. "Just under a foot-and-a-half. River's dropped but not by much."

The current slowed, and the noise subsided. We drifted beside the Bynum Mill, its brick walls standing firm against the encroaching tentacles of kudzu. Mills like this one stood along rivers all across the southern Piedmont. Most were built in the late nineteenth century before the widespread availability of electricity. The natural gradient of the Piedmont rivers, concentrated in one spot through the construction of a dam and millrace, provided the power to run the machinery.

Around these mills, the owners built villages to support the workers, complete with identical woodframe houses, a company store, a Baptist church at one end and a Methodist church on the other. Mill villages were self-contained worlds where everything was taken care of, as long as you didn't cross swords with the owner. Rise up against him, and you were out.

The mills were now shut down, run out of business by cheap foreign labor. I felt sorry for the workers and their families, many of whom had to move to find work. Perhaps it broadened their horizons to move outside these little villages, but leaving home was never easy.

We fanned out four abreast across the Haw, paddling into the late April sun. Talk went back and forth about the Red Clay Ramblers' performance at Cat's Cradle and the new movie at the Carolina Theater. Approaching the phalanx of wooded islands, we turned our attention back to the river.

"Which way, Jim?"

"Middle right should be open at this level."

Below Bynum, the Haw braids into narrow channels that run like trails through the forest. Many of these are impassable at lower water levels, but at a foot-and-a-half, you have many options. This was the first time I'd gone middle right.

Jim led the way into the tunnel of green. Ironwood, river birch, oak, poplar—everything was leafing out. Dogwood blossoms lit the understory. Bluejays called back and forth. We glided fast and silent, the lapping current masking the click of paddle against rock.

A flash of movement caught my eye—something dark sprinting through the underbrush. Suddenly, it sprouted wings and flew up over the channel, so close Cathy could have touched it with her paddle. A wild turkey! Before I could alert Jim and his friends, it soared into the woods on the opposite bank, dodged left and right through the trees and was gone.

Cathy turned, eyes and mouth wide open. I shook my head—river magic.

Jim angled right between a break in the islands, and one by one, we followed, emerging into bright sunlight. The newly widened channel surged over a ledge.

"Rock on left!"

We rode the curving tongue through the rocky maze. Cathy drew on one side; I swept on the other. No time to second-guess. We cleared the last boulder and shipped our paddles, the rapid's loud applause fading behind.

"Awesome!"

"Did you see me clip that rock?"

Gathered at the base of the rapid, we exclaimed about near misses and great moves. Then, it was on to the next rapid.

The Highway 64 bridge loomed ahead. Now the real action began. The tree line fell away to reveal a broad rock-rimmed sweep of river—Ocean Boulevard. Menacing waves ran bank to bank as far as the eye could see. This could be ugly.

We slid into the first set of waves, alternately paddling and freezing as the bow rode up the crests. Water poured over the gunwales and sloshed around my ankles. By the time we'd cleared the second set of waves, the water was up to my thighs.

"Eddy out. We need to bail," I said.

We angled for a boulder on river left with a still pool behind. As the bow crossed the eddy line, the stern swung in a violent arc, yawed and rocked back to level. Heart pounding, I snugged the stern into the sheltering calm and started to bail.

In the 1970s, there were no electric pumps for canoes. You bailed water out by hand, usually with a plastic milk jug cut in half. This was another problem with canoes. At sixteen or seventeen feet in length, they tended to plough through waves instead of ride over them. Water poured in over the gunwales, filling the boat like a bathtub. If you were paddling with kayakers like we were, they had to wait while you bailed.

"O.K., babe," I said when the water was down to an inch. "Let's go."

To get out of an eddy and back into a fast-moving current, you need to paddle upstream until the canoe is entirely out of the still water. Then you turn sideways and lean downstream, letting the current push the boat around. Your instinct is to lean upstream to counter the onrushing current, but instincts are not always right. The current pushes down on the hull. Give it enough purchase, and it will roll the canoe. The way to stay upright is to commit to the lean.

But I was not yet a believer. I held myself level going into the turn. As if a giant hand reached under the hull, the boat started to roll upstream. I grabbed the gunwale, and for an agonizing second thought we could pull it out. But we'd passed the point of no return. I took a quick and fearful breath as the Haw closed over my head.

81

When I broke the surface, Cathy was yards ahead, being swept away by the current. I rolled onto my back in the swimmer's defensive position, arms out and feet up. A flat boulder offered the nearest refuge. I swam with my paddle and dug my fingers into its scalloped face. Cathy found her own boulder just downstream.

As we clung to our separate islands, the canoe drifted away. I figured it was only a matter of seconds before it wrapped around a rock, but Jim raced out from shore and, using the nose of his kayak, drove the canoe into an eddy. At least the boat was saved.

The current was too strong for any of the kayakers to get back to me, so I let go of my rock and drifted down to Cathy. "Are you okay?" I asked.

"Yeah. A little cold."

"I guess they mean it when they say you have to lean downstream."

We waded through the shallows to where Jim held our upside-down canoe. We got the bow up on a rock and, straining against the vacuum of trapped air, lifted the stern and flipped the boat over, draining out the water.

I held the gunwales while Cathy climbed back aboard. Once again, we had to paddle out of an eddy into fast water. This time we both leaned well downstream when we started the turn. It was scary to tilt that boat, to put it right on edge. But you could feel it reach equilibrium with the current. The boat swung around and rocked back to level.

We didn't have long to relax. Gabriel's Bend, the Haw's most intimidating rapid, loomed just ahead. Gabriel's lies in perpetual shadow tucked in a narrow channel between an island and a steep hillside. The gradient drops at the head of the channel, kicking up waves that can run on for fifty yards. When the Haw reaches a gauge height of a foot-and-a-half, the waves are so tall and steep they form troughs or "holes" that can stall or swamp a canoe.

Difficult rapids should always be scouted from shore, especially those like Gabriel's that you can't see until you're right on top of them. We beached the canoes upstream and followed Jim through the twisted trunks of mountain laurel to the head of the rapid. Jim had to yell to be heard above the roar.

"There's a couple of holes in this first set of waves and another over there on the left."

When you scout a rapid, you play out various routes in your head, figuring what moves you need to make to avoid the danger spots. Looking at Gabriel's, it was clear we'd go through at least one of the holes no matter which route we took.

"If we fill up with water, do we just keep it running straight?"

Jim nodded. "Don't forget the pillowed rock."

Oh, yeah, the pillowed rock. At the bottom of the rapid, just before it opened into a sunlit pool, a half-submerged rock straddled most of the channel. Water poured over the rock then curled back on itself, not a good place to get caught. Whatever our situation coming through the holes, we needed to avoid that rock.

I caught Cathy staring hollow-eyed at the rapid. "You'll get psyched out if you look too long," I said.

"Let's just do it."

Seated in the canoe, I went through all the safety precautions, fully inflating the air bag in the middle of the boat, making sure the stern rope was coiled. If we tipped over again, I didn't want to get my feet tangled in a rope. I cinched down my thigh straps and made sure Cathy did the same.

The kayakers shoved off and disappeared around the tip of an island. You couldn't see the rapid until you were in it, and as we rounded the bend, I could see we were too far in the middle, heading right for the big waves.

"Brace!"

Cathy laid her paddle blade flat against the water to stabilize the boat. We plunged into a hole and submarined through the next wave.

"Paddle!"

The canoe labored up the crest and into the second set. Each wave tossed in another bucketful of water. The pillowed rock loomed ahead.

"Draw right!"

The water-logged canoe barely moved.

"Right! Right! Right!"

We were both drawing frantically when we cleared the edge of the rock and raced into the afternoon light. The canoe was filled with muddy water to the seat bottoms but still upright. With delicate strokes, we turned out of the current and toward the sheltering pool.

Gabriel's Bend is as well known for its finish as for the rapid itself. Coming out from behind the base of the island, paddlers enter a wide pool rimmed on the upstream side by a low rock wall that spans the width of the river. Water gushes through the fissures in a thousand rivulets, each with its own arc and timbre. Cathy snugged the boat against the wall. I grabbed the cooler and climbed out on the rocks.

The kayakers had stopped to play in the curling wave below the pillowed rock. They surfed frontwards and sideways, rolled upside-down and popped back up. These guys were like river otters, never so happy as when they were in the water.

I stripped off my wet shirt and laid it on the rocks. Cathy handed me an apple. We sat with our backs to the sun. Below the pool, the Haw braided again among boulders spotted with orange and lime-green lichen. Patches of ground sprouted loblolly pines as thick as temple pillars.

"Man, I love this river," I said. "It's like a good novel. You've got this long build up to Gabriel's Bend and then this great runout to the end."

Jim frowned. "Did you hear about the reservoir?"

"What reservoir?"

"The Army Corp of Engineers is building a dam about ten miles downstream. Part of a flood control project. It's going to bury every rapid from here to the Steel Bridge—Slippery Ledge, S-Turn, the Pipeline..."

I felt dizzy, confused. All of this—the trees, the rocks, the river itself—submerged under a sheet of brown. *We die. The rivers die. How are we to live?*

"They say it'll be another five years before they close the floodgates," Jim said. "Enjoy it while you can."

"Hell, I'm moving to the mountains," one of the kayakers said.

"Yeah, enough of this bullshit."

There was always that possibility. Take it to another town. But I was tired of looking for greener pastures. I liked Chapel Hill, and I liked my girlfriend. Something would come up no matter where you lived, a dagger in the heart. No, I was staying here.

We packed up the boats and paddled slowly across the pool. At this water level, we had our choice of routes—straight ahead over the five-foot drop known as Moose Jaw Falls or left through Harold's Tombstone. Harold's is a dogleg rapid, a narrow slide at the top followed by a sharp right turn. Lurking center stage at the bottom of the slide is a chiseled rock the size and shape of a headstone. Cathy and I had never made a clean run of it, glancing left and right off the headstone and even hit it head-on once. There wasn't enough push to this rapid to make it truly dangerous, but it could put a dent in our canoe.

As we approached the rapid, I reminded Cathy to draw hard right.

"I know, John. That's the fifth time you've told me."

We drifted under the leaning sycamore and started down the chute. The tombstone rushed toward us, water piling against its face.

"Now!"

Cathy stabbed her blade and pulled. I drew hard in the stern, to no avail. We banged against the tombstone and yawed upstream. Violating one of the cardinal rules of paddling, I reached out and shoved us free. Damned if we were going to roll again.

When we cleared the rapid, I let loose. "We hit that thing every time," I said. "You need to draw repeatedly, not just once."

"I drew a bunch of times. You just didn't see it."

I slapped my paddle down across the gunwales and sighed. Maybe that's the way it was going to be with us. Maybe we were always going to hit Harold's Tombstone.

We dropped over Slippery Ledge and angled through the S-Turn. From here on down, it was all fast water, a quarter-mile-long wave train called The Pipeline. We normally glided through this, set a course and let the current carry us along. This time, I wanted something different.

"Hey, let's paddle this as fast as we can," I said. "Get up some real speed."

Cathy gave an eager nod.

They say you need to be moving faster than the current to control your direction. But control was not the issue here. I just wanted to know what it felt like to move as fast as we could, to feel the rush of wind in my face. As we slid into the rapid, I leaned into my stroke. Soon we were going twice the speed of the current. We flew past the rips and bubbles as if they were stuck in place. We were really moving!

We paddled hard until the rapids ended. The surface smoothed, and the bubbles dissolved. Steel Bridge, a truss bridge of classic turn-of-the-century design, loomed on the horizon. This beloved landmark would also disappear with the new lake.

We pulled out on the bank and tossed our paddles into the canoe. Jim and his friends were nowhere in sight. We walked up to the bridge for a better view, leaned against the rusted steel trusses. Muffled shouts rang out above the distant rush of water, upstream where the river emerged from a tunnel of sycamores.

I grinned. "Hear that? They're playing in the rapids."

Cathy smiled wistfully. Was she thinking, like me, that this river running life was too good to last? There was nothing we could do to save the Haw. But I could ask her to marry me, this time for keeps.

Chapter 7
The Allagash

Daylight warmed the orange fabric of the tent and lured me out of my sleeping bag. I pulled back the flap to find that last night's jagged silhouette had become a green ridgeline of spruce fir. Below it, Heron Lake glistened in the morning sun. And at our doorstep, the near end of the lake, stood a small wooden dam from which a river rippled past with barely a sound.

Dennis was already up, coffee cup in hand, staring at the river through wire-rimmed glasses. "Can you believe it? The Allagash!"

I shook my head. "For awhile there, I thought we'd never make it."

The drive from Chapel Hill had been an ordeal—two days and more than a thousand miles, our four-cylinder sedans with the canoes on top buffeted by tractor trailers and buses. The last leg was the worst. After leaving Dennis's Honda at the take-out on the Allagash, we drove to the put in sixty miles down a dirt logging road. As the light faded in the narrow band of sky above the forest and we passed our second hour without seeing a sign, I began to think we were lost. Then the lake and river appeared, glowing like polished pewter in the last light of day.

Dennis' partner, Martha, approached with a girlish smile, her elbows in tight. She shook her fists with excitement. "We're here!"

Cathy emerged from our tent, and together we stood on the bank beaming at the river.

The Allagash Waterway was one of the few rivers in the East where you could canoe for five or six days without encountering any signs of civilization other than a few log bridges. The waterway is actually a chain of rivers and lakes running for almost a hundred miles through the north Maine woods. It's classified as a Wilderness Waterway by the state of Maine, and a Wild and Scenic River by the federal government.

Dennis was the inspiration behind this trip. He and Martha had become good friends of Cathy's and mine in graduate school. We'd canoed all the local rivers together and were looking to expand our horizons. Dennis had researched the Allagash and gotten the necessary permits and maps. This was our chance to explore a legendary river, and for Cathy and me, very possibly our last shot at a big canoe trip before we had kids.

Dennis and I lifted the canoes off the car and set them on the bank. We broke down the tents and stuffed them into the dufflebags. I hadn't been canoe camping since Keewaydin, but the old lessons came back—heaviest pack behind the center thwart, lighter pack in front. The gear had changed since then. Instead of wooden wannigans laden with cans of beef stew, we had a plastic containers filled with airy packages of freeze-dried pasta. The heavy canvas tents and fat cotton sleeping bags had been replaced by backpacking gear you could hold in one hand. The canvas dufflebag was now waterproof rubber. But I still relished the sight of our possessions tucked into the middle of the boat. Everything we needed was right here.

The fast current below Churchill Dam set us on our way. Dennis motioned for me to take the lead. He was a take-charge kind of guy in most respects, but when it came to river running, he deferred to me.

Within a quarter mile, we reached the head of Chase Rapids, labeled on the waterway map as a long Class II. I loved the chatter of small rapids, the white-tipped waves jumping up to greet you.

"Rock straight ahead. Go left."

Cathy moved us away with a few quick draws. I looked back as we passed the suspicious plume of water. Sure enough, there was a jagged hunk of granite underneath. I turned around and raised my paddle, angled to the left. That's the sign for boats to change course. Whether Dennis and Martha didn't see it or didn't know what it meant, I couldn't tell. They bore straight down on the rock. What the hell were they doing?

The canoe hit with a jarring thud and yawed to one side. I thought for sure they were going over, but the canoe rocked back to level. Dennis's bellow rang out. "God damnit, Martha, what are you doing?"

"Oh, shit," I said to Cathy. "There goes the trip."

Martha's voice floated across the water. "I'm sorry, Den. I didn't see it." She sounded just like my mother, soothing, humble, deflecting my father's anger. They focused their attention back on the river, and by the time they pull abreast, they were both smiling.

"We managed to hit the one rock in the river," Dennis laughed.

"Lucky you fiberglassed that nose," I said.

Dennis and I had identical canoes—factory-second Mad River Explorers with soft noses. Like me, he'd done his own repairs, but instead of two layers of fiberglass, Dennis had lathered on four. That left the nose as blunt as a boot heel, not a problem on the whitewater rivers we frequented, but lousy for flatwater. I didn't say anything at the time, but now I worried what would happen when we hit the lakes.

The current remained strong below Chase Rapids, carrying us through the forest at a runner's clip. There was no need to paddle, so I just leaned back and ruddered. *This is it,* I thought; *this is heaven.*

Beneath the rippled surface, a collage of colored stones raced past—olive, cream, and pink—tinted by the faintly bronze lens of the water. The banks were thick with balsam fir and the lighter-hued leaves of paper birch that fluttered pale side up in the breeze.

A flock of ducks swam upstream along the bank. These were new to me—gray backs, bronze-crested heads, hooked beaks. Mergansers! As we came abreast, the ducks craned their necks and scooted forward like toy hydroplanes. I laughed at their needless flight. Hundreds of canoeists paddled this river every summer. How many had to pass before these ducks could understand we were not a threat? Evolution had not conditioned them to take a relaxed attitude toward life.

"Hey, guys, how about we smoke a doobie?" Dennis lifted a plastic baggie between his legs and proceeded to roll a joint. I glanced at the river, uneasy about the prospect of getting high on unfamiliar waters. What the hell? There weren't supposed to be any more rapids, and we had only a few miles to go.

I took a hit, the pungent odor of marijuana dashing the scent of hemlock and pine. The Allagash became a carnival ride.

"This is all right!" I called to Dennis.

All too soon, the current slowed, and the river widened. We had reached the head of Lake Umsaskis. On the far horizon, marshmallow clouds sat above a line of low, green hills. The midday sun had stilled the morning breeze. Time for lunch.

We pulled the canoes together and lashed the center thwarts with a rope. Martha fixed sandwiches and passed them around. I slipped off my sneakers and propped my feet on the dufflebag.

As the canoes bobbed on the gentle swells, I felt myself slipping back into the rhythm of my Keewaydin summer when time was measured by the slow changing of the light and the accomplishment of a few simple goals.

We picked up our paddles and eased on down the lake. The map showed the campsite to be no more than a mile away. No need to paddle hard. A rocky ledge loomed on the eastern shore. That should be it.

We beached the canoes and climbed the gentle grade to the clearing beneath the pines. Half a dozen tent sites and two sets of fire rings stood at opposite ends of the slope. Plenty of room.

Cathy and I picked out a piece of flat ground at the top of the rise and set up the tent. I donned my bathing suit and ambled down to the lake. The ledge looked like a great place for a dive.

Scanning back down the lake, I spotted a fleet of red canoes headed our way, a camp group, no doubt.

I called to Dennis, "Hey, check this out."

The canoes hugged the near shoreline.

"I hope they're not planning on staying here," I said.

Dennis snorted. "They're not. Simple as that."

But the canoes kept on coming. Without so much as a glance in our direction, the paddlers—teenage boys and a pair of counselors—passed right under our noses and pulled up next to our boats. The boys hopped on shore and fanned out across the campground. "I got this site." "This one's ours."

I approached one of the counselors—a twenty-something

guy wearing a felt Fedora. "Excuse me. This is our campsite. We've been here for at least an hour."

He offered a sympathetic smile. "These big campsites are meant to be shared. There's not enough on the river for everyone to have their own."

Dennis glared at him. "If you're staying, we're moving. Come on, John."

I wanted to hear the counselor's response, but found myself following Dennis back up the hill.

"These guys are invading our campsite," he fumed. "Come on, Martha. Let's pack up the tent."

Cathy turned to me for an explanation. I threw up my hands. Just then the counselor appeared. "You guys don't have to do this. We're really not a bad bunch."

"We were hoping to be by ourselves," I said.

The counselor nodded. "I can tell you for a fact there's another couple of parties coming along behind us. We camped with a family last night. Dad was nuts, yelling at his kids. You wouldn't want to get stuck with them."

Cathy sighed. "Let's stay here, John. I don't want to pack all this stuff up."

"Yeah, Den, let's stay here," Martha said.

Dennis looked at me and, finding no support, shook his head. "Whatever you guys want."

"We'll try to keep it quiet," the counselor said. He headed back down the hill, leaving us staring at each other.

"Let's bring all our stuff up here," I said. "I'll get some firewood."

"We'll get dinner going," Martha said.

Dennis bounced the tent stakes in his hand, not yet ready to let go of his anger. I spoke to Cathy with forced bravado.

"Let's get that firewood before these kids do."

As I combed the fringes of the forest, I kept an ear tuned to the campers.

"Hey, Thompson, check this out. I've got the perfect marshmallow stick."

"Screw you. Mine's better than that."

Just like me at Keewaydin.

At dinner, we mollified ourselves with talk of how we would find our own campsite the following night. Our permit was clear about staying only in designated campgrounds, but we would do what we had to in order to get away from this crowd.

Cathy rummaged through the container I'd packed with cookwear. "Did you remember to bring the detergent, John?"

"I think I forgot it."

"You guys have any?"

Martha shook her head.

Cathy glanced down the hill. "Maybe they'll have some."

As the rest of us watched in anticipation, Cathy walked down to the counselor with the felt hat. He reached into a pack and handed something to her. They struck up a conversation. Twenty minutes later, Cathy returned.

"That guy, Ian, is really interesting," she said. "He was a psych major at Boston College. He started out doing social work, then took this job as a counselor. He went to a canoe camp just like you, John. He's paddled this river before."

I glanced at Ian whittling a piece of wood with his sheath knife. He told one of the boys to stop waving his marshmallow stick around. The kid put it down.

The next morning, I walked down to the lake to wash dishes. Ian and I exchanged greetings.

"I hear you paddled this river before," I said.

"About twenty years ago."

"See any wildlife?"

"A couple of moose. If you get out ahead of the other paddlers, you might see some. They wade out to feed on the aquatic grasses."

I hurried back up the hill to tell the others. We broke camp and headed out on the lake.

A cloud front had moved in overnight, rendering the lake a lifeless gray. The absence of sunlight changes your mood when you're out on water. I scanned the shoreline—nothing. I recalled those long days at Keewaydin paddling in silence under sullen skies. I lowered my gaze and slipped into the old mantra— stroke, stroke, stroke.

Over the course of the morning, Dennis and Martha started to fall behind. They were every bit as strong as Cathy and I, so it had to be the canoe. Cathy and I slowed our strokes and waited for them to catch up.

"That nose slowing you down?" I asked Dennis.

"What do you mean?"

"Your patch job. Kind of fat for lake paddling."

Dennis scowled, and I felt stupid for opening my mouth.

By late afternoon, we reached Round Pond. Our campsite lay somewhere in the bay to the east. According to our map, there was supposed to be a fire tower on the hill above. Our plan was to stay two nights, giving us a day to hike up to the tower.

A cave-like opening in the wooded shoreline marked the entrance to the campsite. We beached our canoes and peered into the shadows. A single picnic table and fire ring stood in a clearing surrounded by gray trunks of cedars. The campsite was meant for one group, but who knew what the practice was out here? We flipped the canoes right on the shoreline, their bright red hulls marking the site as occupied and set up camp.

Cathy picked up a handful of small round-tipped cedar needles that covered the ground. "Smell these."

I knelt down and pressed a tent stake deep into the humus. "We'll sleep well tonight."

Several parties of canoes passed by during the afternoon, but none turned into the bay. By evening, it was clear we'd have the campsite to ourselves. We stripped naked and waded into the lake, clutching bars of soap. The bottom was covered with smooth stones.

Martha was the first to duck her head underwater. She rose with water streaming off her dark hair. "It's not bad!"

After the swim, we brought out our sleeping pads and unrolled them against a fat log. Cathy and I snuggled with our feet to the fire. If we were alone, I would make love to her, fingers clutching the soft carpet of cedar.

I woke to the sound of waves lapping against the shore. A fresh breeze had chased the clouds away, giving us a perfect Maine morning. We should have a fantastic view from the fire tower.

The trail headed up behind the campsite, passing through a shadowland of knee-high ferns at the base of the hill. As we gained elevation, cedars gave way to leafy hardwoods. We stopped to pick raspberries beside the trail. Dennis lit a joint.

Today, I was in the mood for getting high. I marveled at the lacey-winged damselflies alighting on the branches. We hiked for a few minutes, then stopped. Started and stopped again.

As the trail leveled out, I peered ahead for signs of the tower. There was a clearing. What the hell was this? The tower was lying on the ground.

A trio of workmen sat eating lunch beside a tracked vehicle.

"What happened to the tower?" I said.

The workman lowered his thermos. "Blew it up."

"When?"

"Last week."

I threw my hands atop my head, turned to face the others.

"Why'd you do that?" Martha said.

"Department of Forestry transferred the waterway to Parks and Lands. Didn't want the liability."

The men continued eating as if this kind of thing happened every day. I examined the cement footings that once anchored the tower. The metal braces were charred and twisted.

"So what are you doing here now?"

The man wiped his sleeve across his mouth. "Puttin' it back."

"Why?"

"Parks and Lands wants it so's people like you can enjoy the view."

Cathy looked befuddled. Dennis broke into an enormous grin. "Nice to know bureaucracy is alive and well in the wilderness," he said.

"Come back next week," the man said. "Should be up."

We turned and slunk back down the trail. As soon as we were out of sight, we fell down laughing.

"Tell me this isn't real," Martha said.

With no other destination in mind, we took the sandwiches out of the pack and passed them around. We tried to eat, but every few seconds, someone would launch into dialogue. "What happened to the tower? Blew it up. What're you doing now? Puttin' it back."

Grape juice dribbled off my beard. Pieces of tuna fish littered the ground.

Back in camp, we paused in front of our tents. The sly look in Dennis's and Martha's eyes told me sex was on the agenda. Cathy and I slipped into our orange cocoon and wiggled out of our clothes. As I rolled onto her, I heard a burst of laughter from across the way. "What're you doing? Puttin' it back."

In the morning, Martha emerged to say that Dennis was sick. He'd thrown up several times and was running a slight fever. I suggested we get help. Martha demurred. "This always happens to him on vacation. He gets stressed out at work, and when he relaxes, his body needs to purge itself."

Cathy and I exchanged crestfallen glances. We had hoped to make it to Allagash Falls that day.

"You guys go ahead," Martha said. "We'll catch up with you tomorrow."

After mild protestations, Cathy and I packed our gear and headed out. It was liberating to be on our own. We didn't have to worry about going too fast. I wasn't tempted to muddy my head with pot. Best of all, we were out early.

At the end of Round Pond, we slipped back into the serpentine channel of the Allagash. The current rose and pushed us along like an old friend. All along the bottom, flattened leaves of yellow-green grass pointed downstream.

My heart leapt. "There's the grass Ian was talking about!"

We rounded the bend, and there was a bull moose. He stood in midstream, antlers swaying back and forth as he worked the grasses loose. I slipped a camera out of my pack and screwed on a telephoto lens. Seen through the viewfinder, the moose looked dangerously close. I held my breath, waiting for just the right moment. Whoosh! He thrust his head out of the water and stared at me, silver droplets streaming from his muzzle. I snapped the picture, wound and snapped another.

We glided so close, I started to worry. What if he charged? But he'd seen the likes of us before. Unhurried, the moose waded ashore. He stopped on the bank and checked us out one last time, then slipped between the alders.

Cathy turned around, beaming. For two years, she'd heard me run on about sneaking up on bears and grappling with beavers. Now, we had a story of our own.

With the sun high overhead, we stopped for lunch on an island in midstream. Cathy peeled an orange and fed it to me. We took off our clothes—she pale as a Degas nude—and tiptoed into the river. I breaststroked into deep water and spun in slow circles. The water lifted my scrotum with a silken hand. I closed my eyes and floated on my back.

Late in the afternoon, we reached the portage for Allagash Falls. The river offered no hint of what was to come, disappearing around the bend as quiet as a millpond. But as soon as we stepped on the bank, I could feel the throbbing coming through the ground. We followed the trail through the forest, the thunder growing as we crested a ledge. We stepped out onto the rocks.

The falls were so bright I had to hold my hand in front of my eyes. Shouts rose above the roar of falling water.

"Look who's here," I said.

On the far side of the river, two familiar-looking boys clambered up the rocks—the campers. It was too much to hope we wouldn't run into them again.

We followed the trail on downhill and came upon a number of campsites, all occupied. I was amazed at how many different people were here—young couples, old couples, a family with kids. We found Ian at a picnic table mixing a bowl of flour. I walked up and slapped him on the back.

"Guess what we saw today?"

In breathless tones, I told him about the moose. "You were right about getting out early."

Ian invited us to camp with him and the boys.

"Why not?" I said.

"And after you put your tent up, get your suits on. The swimming's great."

The boys were lined up on a ledge, jumping into the foamy water below the falls.

"Mind if I join you?" I said.

The last boy turned around. "Hey, Dane. It's those same people."

I stepped to the edge and looked down. It had been a few years since I'd jumped from this height, but the old competitive spirit rose to the fore. I let out a whoop and dived outward. The black water rushed toward me, exploding in a fist of bubbles and noise.

Cathy jumped in after me, and together with the boys, we tried to swim right up to the falls. I flailed my arms, but the current was too strong. One by one, we gave up and drifted downstream.

Back at the campsite, Ian bent over the fire, stirring a pot of stew while keeping en eye on the biscuits in the reflector oven. Cathy and I gladly accepted his invitation to dinner. We were starting to feel like family.

I dug my tin plate out of my pack and stood in line with the campers. I might as well have been fourteen again, peering around their shoulders, worried that I wouldn't get enough. Then that first mouthful of stew went down, and everything seemed right with the world. I leaned back against the tree and watched the feathered clouds in our small patch of sky change from pink to orange to gray.

Ian lit the Coleman lantern and hung it on a nail. He directed a group of boys to gather the dishware and followed them down the darkening trail to the river. The three who remained at the picnic table broke out a deck of cards.

"Wanna join us?" T.J. said.

I shook my head. "Mind if we sit and watch?"

"Sure, come on."

The game was five-card draw with matchsticks as money. A few hands in, it became clear that blond-headed Dane was the master at this game. He upped the ante regardless of what he was holding, fixing the other boys with a cold blue stare. Chase and T.J. folded every time.

Dane scooped up his winnings with a haughty laugh. T.J. reached for Dane's discarded hand. "Let's see your cards."

Dane grabbed them up. "Screw you; I'm not showing 'em."

"Man, you were bluffing!"

"That's for me to know and you to find out."

T.J. tossed his matchsticks across the table. "I quit."

"Me, too," Chase said.

An old anger welled inside me. I remembered being bluffed into submission by that asshole Shephard, thinking that people like him would always come out on top. I wanted to grab the cards out of Dane's hand and expose him as the loser I knew he was. But I stayed quiet.

"How do you guys like camp?" Cathy asked.

"It's okay."

"It's a lot of paddling."

Dane sniffed. "I think it sucks. My Dad sent me here so he could hang out with his new girlfriend."

Dane started sweeping up the spilled flour on the table top with a playing card, forming it into two lines. He took a dollar bill from his pocket, rolled it up and stuck it in his nose. He leaned forward.

Chase guffawed. "Are you crazy?"

"Do it," T.J. said.

Dane stared at me, waiting. I'd never met the cold eyes of an angry fourteen-year-old, never imagined a boy could know about cocaine. It wasn't my place to discipline him. It wasn't me he was angry with. He would have to make the next move.

"Just kidding," he said.

Ian returned and put the dishes on the table. "O.K., guys, time for bed."

Whining in protest, the boys shuffled back to their tents.

"Want me to leave the lantern on?" Ian asked.

"No, thanks," I said. "We're heading off to bed."

Ian shut off the light, and the world went black. But as if someone had popped a flashgun in my face, I saw an after-image—Dane, staring at me with a dollar bill up his nose. He was everywhere—in the woods, in the sky.

I reached for Cathy's hand under the table. She gave me a squeeze. I knew what she was thinking. We'd been married now for two years. The time was coming soon. The thought of having a baby, any baby, was scary enough. But what if we were dealt a losing hand? What if we got Dane?

In the morning, Cathy and I waited at the head of the falls for Dennis and Martha. Below, the other parties were packing up and heading downstream. We would see no moose today.

Dennis and Martha arrived around noon. Dennis had fully recovered, and they were eager to head on to the takeout at Twin Brook. We ate a hurried lunch and portaged around the falls.

The afternoon was hot and windless. A chainsaw whined in the distance, growing louder at every turn. Then came the growl of a bulldozer. The Allagash brochure described the "Wilderness Waterway" as extending only a short distance back from the river. Beyond that, commercial logging was permitted. This so-called wilderness was just an illusion. Reality lay beyond the thin veil of trees.

Mile by mile, the river grew wider and shallower. Up ahead, I spotted one of the groups that set off before us. They were out of their boats, dragging them across a gravel bar. I stood up and scanned the river.

Having spent many summer days canoeing down the ankle-deep Chagrin, I'd became an expert at reading shallow water. I knew at a glance where my boat could sneak through and where it would hang up.

"Over there," I pointed. "Along the bank."

We poled past the stranded canoeists, their faces tired and worn. We passed the family and the older couple, both hard aground. The river was played out, and so were we. Time for the trip to end.

A cluster of parked cars appeared on the left bank.

"There it is," Dennis called. "We've made it."

We ran the canoes onto the bank and exchanged high fives. Then we set about unloading the gear and cramming it into the back of Dennis's Honda. I tied the boats on the roof rack and scrunched in the back seat with Cathy. Now for that awful drive back to the put-in.

I'd been dreading the three-hour shuttle, especially the last sixty miles. But after four days on the river, I was exhausted. I leaned my head against the window and quickly fell asleep.

The rumble of wheels on gravel stirred me awake. The car slowed to a halt. Dennis turned around in the front seat. "The canoes are sliding off," he said. "We need to retie the ropes."

I hauled myself out and helped Dennis shove the canoes back on the rack. I picked at one of the knots, but it wouldn't budge.

"Thing's stuck," I said.

"You need to retie it."

I tried but couldn't loosen the knot. "The canoes aren't going anywhere," I said. "Even if the gunwale slides off the edge, the rope will keep them on."

Dennis frowned.

"I'm telling you, they aren't coming off," I said.

We climbed back in the car and headed on through the forest. Finally, we broke into the clearing. There was Heron Lake and Churchill Dam. We were all cheering when Dennis hit the pothole. The car bounced, a loud whack followed. Dennis skidded to a halt. For an instant, no one spoke. The windows on my side of the car were crackling, breaking into ever smaller pieces. Beneath the canoe that hung off the roof, I could see the Allagash rippling into the forest, fragmenting until it was nothing more than a blur.

Chapter 8
The Rocky

In the spring of 1982, Cathy came out of the bathroom holding the pregnancy kit. "It's positive," she said.

For a long minute, neither of us spoke. We'd been trying to get pregnant for almost a year, but now that it had happened, we thought of all the reasons this wasn't a good time. Cathy would have to cancel her family planning workshop in Nairobi. There would be no canoe trip to the Boundary Waters.

"I guess there's never going to be a perfect time," Cathy said. "We just have to accept that things are going to be different."

Her body was the first thing to change. She lost her tapered waist, her slender arms. But her face flushed with expectant pride; her breasts became a young man's dreams. Even her belly struck me as beautiful, until she began to feel pain.

At sixteen weeks, we went to the hospital for a check-up. Cathy's ligaments hurt, and she seemed to be swelling faster than normal. Dr. Sims had her lie on the examining table and ran the ultrasound wand across her belly. Two fuzzy shapes appeared on the monitor, facing each other like yin and yang.

"You've got twins," he said. "Boys."

My stomach dropped. One child was what we had planned. One I could handle. But two meant a total loss of freedom. Twins owned their parents.

"Something else is going on here," he said.

Dr. Sims recentered his wand.

"This fetus is smaller than the other. It could have something to do with your swelling, improper circulation of amniotic fluid. We're going to have to watch it."

* * *

The spring before Cathy became pregnant, the rains fell hard across the Piedmont, sending rivers out of their banks. While the big ones became too dangerous to paddle, smaller rivers actually became runnable for the first time. Such was the case with the Rocky.

More hissing stream than river, the Rocky is unnavigable for most of the year. A long-legged girl could wade across the boulder-strewn channel without getting her shorts wet. But when heavy rains turn the Haw into a muddy conveyor belt, the Rocky becomes a first class whitewater run.

I picked up the phone and called Dennis, asking if he and Martha would like to join us on a run of the Rocky.

"We're taking your car, right?" he said.

Over the past year, Dennis had forgiven me my sins and the four of us were back to running rivers together. They agreed to meet us at ten.

After loading our canoe on the Capri, Cathy and I drove through the winding roads to the remote southwestern corner of Chatham County. We arrived at the tiny concrete bridge and pulled over to the shoulder, where Dennis and Martha waited. Together, we walked onto the bridge and peered upstream where the Rocky swirled out of the forest. "Looks a good bit higher than last time," I said. "At least a foot."

We had done the Rocky only once before, several years past. My memory of the rapids was vague. There was a broken dam about halfway down and a big drop just beyond.

"Do you remember how to get to the put-in?" Martha asked.

I glanced down the road curving through the pastures. "Take a left at the church and another left somewhere after that. I'll find the way."

Twenty minutes later, we were at the put-in, sliding the canoes in the river. Cathy pulled the thigh straps over her legs and playfully rocked the boat. I was surprised at how relaxed she was, trusting that we could face whatever came along. I, for one, was nervous.

"You guys stay close," I said to Dennis and Martha. "If one of us gets in trouble, the other needs to be there to help."

As we shoved off the bank and entered the narrow channel, twisting, I rose up on my knees. The current drew us toward the first bend and the sound of falling water. The rapid came into view, a slide between two rocks.

"Draw left!"

Cathy and I switched sides in unison. The boat moved with us. As we rode down the V, the boat hit a submerged rock and shuddered to a crawl. But it slid right off and kept on moving, nothing but a little red paint left behind.

I loved this boat with its tough ABS hide. The bottom was streaked and gouged in a hundred places, but it never seemed to crack. The nose I'd refiberglassed several times, but that was to be expected. You can't hit a rock head on and not expect to pay the price.

The Rocky snaked on through the forest, never affording a long view. I tried to gauge the size of the unseen rapids by the sound—a hiss, a rush, a roar.

"Far right!"

Dennis and Martha followed close behind, Dennis's commands echoing my own. Every now and then I heard his basso reassurance. "Doing great, Martha."

The rapids kicked up higher the farther we went. A line of truncated saplings appeared in mid-river. Something wasn't right about that.

"Here's the dam! Get to shore!"

* * *

Through the second trimester and on into the third, Cathy's belly continued to swell, her skin stretched so tight it hurt her to touch it. Dr. Sims called it acute hydramniosis, the uncontrolled production of amniotic fluid. Cathy wondered aloud how much she could take, turned a tearful eye to the wall.

Each week, we returned to the hospital where Dr. Sims brought out his magic wand. "This one's normal size," he said of the larger fetus. "The other's hardly grown. My guess is that the smaller one will die before it comes to term. In that case, it will kill the other one, too."

The words seemed to come from another planet.

"Are you paying attention, John?" Dr. Sims said. "I see this glazed look in your eye."

"Yes, I'm listening."

He turned back to the monitor, the image coming in and out of focus. "Your fundus is also much larger than it should be at

108

five months," he said to Cathy. "If the swelling continues, it will start to affect your breathing. That could be dangerous."

Cathy spoke in her calm, professional voice. "What can we do?"

Dr. Sims shook his head. "The only way to eliminate the threat is to terminate the pregnancy. But that's a decision for you all to make."

* * *

We ran the canoes into the alders and clambered across the ledge. The last time we were here, the dam stood clear of the river, water funneling through a break on the left-hand side. Now the river thundered over an invisible hump. Yard-high tail waves ran on for fifty yards, roiling, ugly.

"I think we need to walk this one," I said.

Dennis nodded. "Good call."

I hated to bypass a rapid. If I were paddling solo, I'd run it without question. But tandem paddlers would definitely swamp. I walked back to the canoe, grabbed the bowline, and started jerking the boat over the rocks.

"Take it easy," Cathy snapped. "I'm trying to help you lift it."

I stopped pulling and waited for Cathy to grab hold of the stern. Why was I doing this? The times we're most afraid are when we need to stick together. No one put you in this situation, so don't blame someone else.

The fast water continued around the bend toward what looked like another big drop. The near bank was tangled with driftwood—no chance to scout. We'd have to run this one blind.

A narrow chute promised a way through, but as we neared the edge, the river fell away.

"Brace!"

We teetered downward into a hole.

"Paddle!"

We rose on the far side with a boatful of water. "Eddy out. We've got to bail!"

There was no slack water to snug into. The bank was steep and brushy. As we swung into shore, Cathy grabbed a branch and held on tight. I started bailing. Dennis and Martha swung in hard beside us.

"Watch your fingers!" I yelled.

The boats clanged together.

* * *

We scheduled the abortion for the following week. The nurse ushered Cathy into a private room. Dr. Sims gave her prostaglandin to bring on labor. He said it would take effect in two to three hours.

I'd come to despise this hospital with its airless rooms, its sick and dying patients. I asked if I could go out for lunch, promising to return in an hour. Cathy picked up a book and waved me out the door.

Downtown Chapel Hill looked just as it did the day I arrived. Students strolled the brick sidewalks in cut-off jeans and flip-flops. But their carefree laughter rang flat. They had no clue what lay ahead.

I ate a burger on Franklin Street, then headed back to the hospital. As I stepped off the elevator, a nurse hurried past.

"She's already in labor," the nurse said. "I'll buzz the doctor."

I followed in behind and took Cathy's hand. She squeezed hard and cried out.

Dr. Sims arrived and looked under the sheets. "You're going to need to step outside," he said to me.

I waited in the hall. Cathy's cries mingled with the soothing reassurances of doctor and nurse. After a prolonged silence, Sims emerged carrying a plastic bucket.

The boys lay on their sides in a pool of clear liquid and blood. Their arms were bent, hands curled as if holding something—a blanket, a paddle. Their journey on earth was over.

* * *

The rock loomed about twenty yards ahead, partially hidden by the wave that pillowed against its backside. We could have dodged it easily if I'd called it out. We could have made it home. But I decided to keep quiet. I was tired of always being the one to give orders, to be on the lookout for trouble. I wanted to see how long it would take Cathy to react. We bore down on the rock—10 yards, 9, 8...

"Draw right!" I screamed.

We hit the rock amidships and swung sideways to the current. Water poured over the upstream gunwale; the boat began to roll. Cathy tumbled into the river and was washed downstream. To my left was the rock, high and dry in the shadow of the boat. I stepped onto it and watched the disaster unfold.

The canoe held together for maybe three seconds while the current surged against the hull. With the sound of a log being split by a maul, the wooden gunwales snapped. The hull collapsed and wrapped around the rock. My canoe was destroyed.

Dennis and Martha raced past, headed after Cathy. I heard her cry out, saw her jerk sideways as she bounced off an unseen

111

rock. I watched all this standing on my little island in the middle of the raging current. Nothing touched me. I could stand there forever.

After helping Cathy ashore, Dennis and Martha pulled their canoe back up the bank and paddled out to rescue me.

"Come on, John," Dennis said, as I stared at our pinned canoe, now the shape of a horseshoe. "You'll never get it out until the river drops."

I stepped into their boat and squatted behind the center thwart. As they paddled downstream, I gripped the gunwales with both hands helpless as a child.

Cathy huddled on shore, rubbing her bloodied leg. I asked if she was hurt.

She winced. "I banged up my stupid knee."

"Can you walk? It's only a little way."

"I guess so."

Two days later, we came back for the canoe. We waded into the now subdued waters, pried the canoe off the rock, dragged it through the woods, and hoisted it onto the roof of the car where it sat like a ruptured banana.

"It's ruined," I said.

But ABS has a remarkable memory, as they say in the plastics trade. On Jim East's advice, we set the boat on saw horses and weighed the ends down with cinderblocks. Slowly, the hull regained its old shape, better than I'd ever have imagined. I clamped on new gunwales, screwed them together, sanded them smooth. When it was all done, the canoe still bore a wrinkle around the middle, a reminder of our past, but it paddled straight and true.

Chapter 9
The Chattooga

Two years after her abortion, Cathy gave birth to a healthy eight-pound boy. We named him Jackson, in part because of my fond memories of my father calling me by that nickname in his lighter moments.

"Hey, Jackson. What's up?"

Dad didn't like it. When we returned to Gates Mills that summer, he mumbled something about giving my son a "Negro name."

"You don't ever remember calling me 'Jackson'?" I asked.

Dad looked away. He was upset that I hadn't named my son "John," thereby breaking a tradition that stretched back at least five generations. His disgust with my son's name came on top of his bad-mouthing my decision to live in the South (Land of Losers), to marry Cathy (family not in the Social Register), and to paint our new house gray instead of colonial white as required by architectural code in Gates Mills. Dad delivered his assessment of Cathy's family, whom he'd never met, after sitting down on the patio with his second martini. He spoke matter-of-fact, as if discussing my plans for buying a new car.

"I look for someone whose father is a lawyer or doctor. Maybe a minister."

"You're right, Dad," I said. "I think I'll go for the Muffy instead of the Cathy."

I wanted to leap out of the L.L. Bean lawn chair and strangle him. But Manuels never hit. Manuels never touched. I held my tongue, felt the burner ignite, blood boiling to the roots of my too-long hair.

* * *

For more than a year after Jackson's birth, the canoe stayed in the garage. Cathy was nursing and couldn't afford to take a day off. Jim, Dennis and Martha all moved away, so I didn't have any pals I could call on for canoeing. But who needed to canoe when you had this amazing new person in the house?

At the age of a few months, Jackson seemed to understand humor and jest. For him I played the funny man, popping up from behind couches, putting grapes in my eyes.

As soon as Jackson could hold himself upright, I hoisted him on my shoulders and carried him into the woods. I pointed out the bluejays and squirrels, the hawk circling overhead. His small hands pounding on my head told me he'd seen them.

I dreamed of the day when I could take Jackson out on the rivers. I'd do it differently than my father. I'd bring him along step by step, encouraging him all the way. We'd become a real team, paddling all the rivers together. When the time came that he wanted to paddle on his own, I wouldn't hold him back.

To be able to spend more time with Jackson, I quit my job with the state and joined an alternative energy research agency in the nearby Research Triangle Park. My new officemate welcomed me with a firm handshake.

"Are you a canoeist?" I asked, seeing the photos on his desk of a boat in whitewater.

"Every chance I can get."

"Where's this one taken?"

"Devil's Kitchen on the Maury."

The sight of Keith's burly, bearded frame up to his chest in whitewater gave me pause.

"You must be pretty good," I said.

"I paddle with a bunch of guys who mostly like to have fun. You ought to come with us on our next trip."

"Where are you headed?"

"Chattooga. Section III."

Guidebooks divide the Chattooga River into four sections. Section IV is the toughest—a stunningly beautiful and truly dangerous run with waterfalls and undercut rocks that have trapped and drowned dozens of boaters. Section III has its own beauty and more than enough challenges for tandem canoeists. For thirteen miles along the Georgia-South Carolina border, the river tumbles through a rocky gorge with more than a dozen Class III rapids, three class IVs, and an infamous Class V—Bull Sluice.

Cathy and I had canoed this section years before, running everything except the Bull. She had no qualms about walking that rapid. One glance at the boat-eating hydraulic, and she was on her way across the portage. I wavered for half-an-hour before chickening out. This time, maybe I'd do it.

I rendezvoused with Keith and his friends at the Burger King parking lot in Chapel Hill. They seemed like a friendly bunch—

George, Michael, Roger, and Keith's wife, Karen. We piled into Keith's van and drove five hours to set up basecamp in the Sumter National Forest. The next morning, we parked at the Earl's Ford trailhead and carried the three canoes down the long, steep path to the river.

The Chattooga looked beautiful in the morning sunlight. Ale-colored water flowed over a bed of sand sparkling with flecks of mica. I set the Explorer on a sandbar and went through the usual preparations, clipping the throw bag and bailer to the rear seat, the waterproof dry bag with my change of clothes to the thwart, and stowing the extra paddle under the center air bag. I fastened my helmet and Velcro-wristed gloves, picked up my paddle, and glanced around at my trip mates.

Keith and Karen were ready to go. Seated in their yellow canoe, Karen pointed to each item on their checklist as Keith called it out. These two knew what they were doing.

George, meanwhile, walked around the beat-up canoe he dubbed "the Freighter," trying to figure out where to stick his cooler. He had won me over on the drive down, teasing the waitress at the diner where we stopped for lunch. "Some people call me the Wolfman," he told her in a deep baritone, stroking his brown goatee. Then leaning back to pat his ample belly, he added, "But you can call me the Doughboy."

George would be paddling the Freighter with Michael. Eventually. Six-foot-two and built like Superman, Michael seemed paralyzed by the decision about which of his several changes of clothes to keep in his mesh duffle and which to put in his dry bag. For minutes at a time, he'd stare at an individual item as if it might speak to him.

I dug my paddle in the sand and glanced at the sun. Already it was above the ridgeline. At this rate, we wouldn't get to Bull

Sluice before evening. And Roger, where the hell was Roger?

"Hey, Keith, have you seen my bowman?" I asked.

"Probably forgot something. He'll show up eventually."

At length, Roger emerged from the trail, eyes downcast. "I think I forgot my lifejacket. Would anyone happen to have a spare?"

Keith rolled his eyes and threw him the keys to the van. "There's one in the back. Did you bring a paddle?"

"No."

"Jesus Christ, Roger. What did you remember?"

Half an hour later, Roger returned with life jacket and paddle. He offered me a sheepish smile. "Keith says you and me are together."

"Do you mind taking bow?" I asked.

"The bow works fine for me," he said.

After Roger got himself settled, we pushed off the sandbar and rode the gentle current around the bend. Section III starts out nice and easy, but I always feel a drumbeat of fear. Once you round that first bend, there's no turning back. There are no roads or houses for the next thirteen miles, and it's a long hike out if for any reason you have to get off the river. This was not a run where I wanted to be paired with a stranger, but there seemed to be no choice.

"War Woman coming up," Keith called.

War Woman is a double ledge with drops of about a foot each. You have to take the second drop at an angle to avoid a rock at the bottom, but it's nothing a decent paddler can't manage. As we slid over the first ledge, I called out for a right hand draw. Roger hesitated.

"Right!" I said.

Roger made a feeble stab. Too late. We glanced off the rock and yawed hard to the side.

"Jesus Christ, man!"

"Sorry! Sorry!"

This was bad. If we had trouble on War Woman, what would happen at Dick's Creek, Second Ledge, Bull Sluice ... I missed not having Cathy in the bow. She was strong and quick.

Beyond War Woman, the current slowed. Sunlight flashed off the rippling water. The air lay warm and still. High on the ridgetop, leaves fluttered in a silent breeze.

A gunshot rang out downstream. Keith stopped paddling. "What the hell was that?"

"Sounded like a .22," I said.

The Chattooga, of course, is famous for having been the site where John Boorman filmed the 1972 classic *Deliverance*. I knew better than to think that this river was actually prowled by sadistic rednecks waiting to sodomize hapless boaters. Still, the man in the coveralls standing on the bank was most definitely not an actor. And the pistol he held was definitely not a toy.

Keith offered a solemn nod, to which the man responded with a barely noticeable jerk of his blue-capped head. He was staring into the water, looking at what I couldn't tell.

"How ya doin' this morning?" George called.

"Awright."

"What're you up to?"

"Tryin to shoot me some fish."

"Having any luck?"

"Seen a few. Can't seem to hit 'em."

Shooting fish? It was all I could do to hide my disdain. But George carried on as if this was the kind of thing he saw every day.

"I hear shock waves'll stun fish. If you graze 'em with a bullet, do they float to the top?"

The man drew a hand over his grizzled chin. "Well, there's them that do and them that don't."

George nodded. "Have a good day!"

As soon as we were out of sight, we circled the boats. Karen broke into a huge grin. "Are you kidding me? That guy was right out of central casting."

Michael squeeled. "Weee! Weee!"

George dropped into a lower register. "Well, there's them that do and them that don't."

I felt the morning's tension flee with the raucous laughter. It was a sunny day, and I was back on the water.

The Appalachians are among the world's oldest mountains, formed eons ago by the repeated collisions of the North American, Eurasian, and African continents. As gentle and rolling as the Appalachians are today, the violence of those events is hard to imagine. Entering the second mile of the Chattooga, there's no denying that something cataclysmic happened.

Giant slabs of rock shoot upward from the riverbed, some tilted at crazy angles. The Chattooga whispers through this graveyard, humbling paddlers into silence. If the foundation of the Earth could be thrust open like this, what else could happen? We posed for pictures and headed downstream.

The current picked up speed, running us along the leafy wall of alder bushes and mountain laurel. I loved the sensation of whisking down a gentle grade, paddle held just so as to keep the stern in line.

The river stilled and widened as if backed behind a dam. I detected a line against the wooded horizon.

Dick's Creek Ledge is very much like a broken dam—a sheer unrunnable (except in high water) drop on the right hand side of the river, but a double drop on the left. The current pours through a natural dip in the ledge, races across a small pool, and turns at right angles as it piles up against an elongated rock. To avoid that rock, the paddler must execute a forty-five degree turn at high speed, banking off the watery pillow and riding down a narrow V-shaped chute. It's not a dangerous rapid, but it is tricky and always needs to be scouted.

We beached our canoes on the lip of the ledge, worn smooth and round as the back of a whale. Keith pointed out the route, telling Karen she needed to make a "fierce" right hand draw to avoid the pillowed rock.

Karen frowned. "I'll do a draw. I don't know how fierce it'll be."

They settled into their canoe and paddled into the still water above the ledge. I liked the way Keith and Karen had outfitted their boat. Instead of seats, they'd installed foam saddles that kept them low to the water. They sat perfectly upright and kept their movements to a minimum.

As they slid through the break in the ledge, Karen reached out and planted her paddle. The canoe jumped to the right, banked off the pillowed rock, and rode down the chute on a level plane.

I turned to Roger. "Did you see how they did that?"

"I think so."

"You need to do a solid draw."

"Right. Right."

As we paddled upstream, I glanced over my shoulder, keeping my eye on the center of the V.

"You ready?"

"I guess so."

I turned the boat and paddled to the edge. The current grabbed hold, pulled us down the V and shot us toward the pillowed rock.

"Draw right!"

I backwatered hard. The canoe turned as if on rails and dropped into the chute. I was marveling at our success when the canoe canted upstream and flipped over. Face and hands pressed to the slimy rock, I slid down the chute underneath the canoe and splashed to a halt in the pool. Two hard kicks, and my legs came free of the thigh straps. I stood up in the waist-deep water next to Keith and Karen's canoe.

"You guys all right?" Keith asked.

Roger looked shell-shocked, his rain suit plastered to his body. "A little banged up, but I'll survive."

"John?"

"Fine." I didn't know what had just happened, but it must have been Roger's fault. This had the makings of a disaster.

Not wanting to repeat our mishap, George and Michael decided to take a "cheat route" over the ledge. They lined the Freighter up on the very edge of the V and not surprisingly ran aground. Refusing to get their feet wet, they stayed in their seats and inch-by-inch rocked the boat forward.

"Jesus Christ, guys, get out of the fucking boat!" Keith said.

George paused in his rocking. "Never disturb the Doughboy in the midst of his training."

Minutes later, they slid to a halt in the lower pool. George and Michael raised their arms in victory. Keith and Karen broke into applause. It took me a moment to overcome my offended sensibilities, to realize this wasn't a game of one-upsmanship. These guys were here to have fun. They were all friends, and I wanted to be part of it.

Beyond Dicks Creek, the hills that had sloped back from the river's edge suddenly loomed high and close. Dark spears of hemlock mingled with the paler crowns of poplar and oak. The river slowed and tapered, gathering itself for a charge through the canyon known as The Narrows.

The entrance to The Narrows is marked by offsetting angled slabs of rock that constrict the Chattooga to half a dozen yards. A white tongue drops into a deep hole that will spill a canoe if you hit it wrong. Roger and I made a clean run and bounded through the tail wave. Undulating walls of metamorphic rock closed in on both sides. The river blossomed with swirls and boils, specks of mica flashing in the depths.

Keith spotted a crescent of sand along the south-facing wall and recommended we stop for lunch. We beached the canoes and stepped onto the clean white surface. There wasn't a single footprint, not even any animal tracks. We were the first ones on the sandbar since the water dropped in the spring.

I pulled out my plastic bottle and took a long drink of water. Michael passed around a bag of gorp.

"Anyone care for some Honey Bun?" George said.

Keith snarled. "Get that thing away from me."

George devoured the mitten-sized pastry, moaning with feigned delight.

"Now for the main course," he said. From his cooler, George brought out a prepackaged luncheon tray. He peeled back the plastic cover and pointed out the offerings. "Here you have your basic Ritz cracker with peanut butter. And over here, medallions of baloney. The dessert is some kind of mystery pudding. I just love that bright yellow dye."

"George, you are the anti-Christ," Michael said.

Now that we were on the river, I warmed up to Michael. He was utterly without pretense, full of enthusiasm and good humor. Roger, too, seemed remarkably upbeat, given the morning's rocky start. He inquired about my work and family, taking special interest in Jackson.

"I've got twin boys—four year-olds," he said. "When Jackson gets a little older, we'll have to get them together."

Karen seemed totally at ease in the company of men. In a loud, husky voice, she recounted the highlights of the morning's run. "Michael, you and George carved out a whole new route down Dick's Creek Ledge. They need to put that one in the guidebooks."

"At least we made that turn," Michael said.

Keith, always brutally honest, interjected. "You sucked is what you did."

Michael laughed. "You're right, Keith. We did suck."

We paddled out of The Narrows in high spirits. As the river widened and slowed, a break in the horizon marked the second of the big drops. Second Ledge mirrors Dicks Creek from above, but instead of falling in stages, it drops all at once—seven feet straight down.

I asked Roger if he was up for running it. He declined but gladly offered to take my picture. I was humbled once again.

Like a first jump off a diving board, the worst part about running Second Ledge is the anticipation. I paddled to the edge several times and retreated. Cheered on by Roger, I finally decided to commit. The drop was over in a second. I landed with a gentle thud in the aerated pool, arms upraised in victory.

Keith and Karen followed, approaching with steady strokes and landing perfectly. If either of them was surprised, they didn't show it. George and Michael looked good going over the ledge, but their combined weight did them in on the landing. As Roger clicked away with his camera, the Freighter nosed underwater and rolled. George bobbed to the surface, water dripping off his goatee. "I want that roll of film, Roger."

For every rapid with a name, there is another stretch of

whitewater on the Chattooga that dazzles with its beauty. The current rippled over gravel bars and banked off monoliths of metamorphic rock. Ancient hemlocks with open understories give tantalizing glimpses into the shady forest. And the high hills change hue as the sun begins its downward arc toward afternoon.

As the day went on, Roger paddled with growing confidence, his strokes quick and sure. We rode the big waves at the bottom of Rollercoaster, dashed through the opening at Eye of the Needle, and skirted the big rock at the bottom of Keyhole.

In the eleventh mile, my energy began to flag. The glare of the low sun, the stress and heat were taking its toll. The river slowed; conversation dwindled. We were all thinking the same thing.

"We gonna run the Bull, George?" Michael asked.

"Don't know. Have to give it a look."

A cluster of boats—yellow, orange, green, and red—appeared on the shore, their paddlers nowhere to be seen. We beached our canoes, unclipped our throw bags, and followed the sandy path through the rocks.

You hear Bull Sluice before you see it, a dull throb that vibrates through the bedrock. Paddlers stand along the shore, heads canted downward, faces gone slack. I stepped to the top of the ledge and froze, hit by a wall of sound. A dozen feet below, the Chattooga swirled inside a rock-rimmed cauldron, deep, black, and menacing. The cauldron was fed by a crystal sheet of water pouring over a five-foot ledge and spinning back on itself at the base. You look at it and think, "This is where I could die."

Keith appeared beside me. "I always think this thing isn't going to look as bad as I remembered it, but it's always worse."

As the rest of our crew gathered to watch, a canoe bobbed down the narrow channel and into the pool just above the ledge. The channel comes in at right—angles to the ledge, and it's nearly impossible to make the turn without eddying out to slow your momentum. But the pool is small, and if you don't complete the turn, you're in big trouble.

The canoeists started their turn, aiming for the sheltered water behind a boulder on the far shore. The stern swung in an arc just above the ledge. Faced away from the drop, the paddlers could not see how close they were, and when the current grabbed hold, it was too late. The canoe slid backwards over the ledge and capsized. Boat and paddlers surfaced in the cauldron, swirled once around the bowl and shot out the narrow chute.

"That's it," Karen said. "I'm walking."

Roger nodded. "Ditto for me."

I stared at the rapid, felt my stomach start to knot. "I'll run it if you will, Keith."

Keith nodded. "How about you, Michael?"

Michael conferred with George. "We could possibly run this straight through if we stay to the inside. What do you think?"

"Beats trying to eddy out the Freighter."

Keith and I offered to man the throw ropes if George and Michael would go first. As they headed back up the trail, I loosened the draw string on the yellow nylon bag. Coiled inside lay fifty feet of bright orange rope. By holding onto one end of the rope and tossing the bag toward the river, you could extend a lifeline to someone trapped in a hydraulic or being swept downstream. But the toss has to be right on the money. There's no catching up to a rope in a raging current.

Minutes passed before the Freighter came around the bend riding the swift current. George and Michael looked grim as prisoners going to the gas chamber. They hugged the inside of the narrow channel, but were still at an angle approaching the ledge.

Keith frowned. "They're fucked."

The canoe flipped on landing, tossing its passengers into the swirling waters. I readied my throw rope, but George and Michael swept past, eyes locked on the sluice. They flushed out the giant spigot like so many specks of dirt, slowed to a halt and swam to shore.

The Freighter was not so lucky. Sucked sideways into the hydraulic at the base of the ledge, it spun around and around and finally disappeared. From deep within the bowels of the cauldron came the hollow thud of a plastic hull being kicked and gored. For long seconds, it remained out of sight, then to the exclamations of the watching crowd, erupted skyward like a breaching whale. It splashed down and washed out the chute, drifting upside-down among the sticks and leaves.

Keith volunteered to go next. He was barely gone five minutes before appearing at the head of the entry rapid. Keith does things by the book, so I was not surprised when he chose to eddy out above the ledge. He turned the canoe with unhurried strokes, keeping well away from the ledge. After pausing to catch his breath against the far shore, he paddled back out into midstream. Three, four, five strokes, he waited until he was positioned right in the middle. Then, he swung the boat around and headed toward the ledge. Keith's landing was perfect, but for just a moment on impact, he hesitated. The canoe yawed sideways and rolled.

I expected Keith to pop right up, but all I could see was a blur of foam. Then, a hand reached above the surface, twisting and turning. I tossed the bag, but the current snatched it away. By the time Keith surfaced, both were on their way out the chute.

I scrambled along the shoreline and caught up to Keith in the slack water.

"Goddamn Bull," he said.

Now, I was plenty scared. But I saw what had to be done—hit that ledge and paddle like hell.

Dizzy with fear, I headed back to the put in. There was still time to quit. But I wasn't walking away a second time. I was the soldier stepping into the landing craft on his way to Omaha Beach, the Masai boy huddled in a dark hut on the eve of initiation. What drove me forward, I couldn't say. Maybe I had something to prove to my father, something to prove to my friends. But mostly, I wanted to run Bull Sluice.

Before taking the field for my high school soccer team, I would loosen up on the sidelines, run in place, twist my body from side to side. Coach Molten would call from the bench, "Get out there and light a fire, Manuel." Alone at the put-in, I went through the same routine, taking deep breaths, pumping myself up. Then, I climbed in the canoe and pushed off.

An observer on the shore can easily recall a boater's progress through a rapid—the narrowly missed boulder, the canoe plunging through the waves, water streaming from the hull. For the paddler, it's all a blur—flashes of light and shadow, a rush of wind and noise. But I do remember riding out the chute of Bull Sluice and shaking the canyon walls with a magnificent Rebel yell.

Chapter 10
The Nantahala

George threw a stick on the fire and settled into his camp chair. "John, tell the one about the time you nearly blew up your Dad's garage."

Roger handed me the Jim Beam. I took a swig and passed it to Michael, "When I was a kid, one of my weekly chores was to take the garbage out to the garage and burn it in the incinerator," I said. "This one summer had been really humid, and the stuff just wouldn't burn. Dad kept this can of gasoline next to the mower ..."

In the glow of the firelight, faces began to smile. I loved telling these stories, recounting the ways I'd pissed off my father by playing the fool. Best of all was seeing my ten-year-old son leaning forward in his chair, grinning in anticipation of another secret revealed.

I didn't worry that Jackson would some day turn on me. We were close, as close as father and son could be. I read to him every night, coached him in soccer, cared for him when Cathy was overseas on month-long work trips. We could talk about anything.

Almost since the day Jackson was born, I dreamed of introducing him to the canoeing life, to the joys of camping and the company of men. George's son, Jacob, had canoed with us for almost five years before going off to college. Roger and Michael had brought their sons along on several weekend outings. No doubt Keith and Karen's four-year-old, Christopher, would join us one day.

Since Christopher's birth, Karen had abandoned overnight canoe trips, as Cathy had done with Jackson and now our second child, Allison. I missed not having Cathy along, but she was happy for me to have a weekend with "the guys" and to bring Jackson into the fold. She had witnessed the estrangement between me and my father and didn't want it repeated.

Jackson pulled a burning marshmallow from the fire and held it to his face. He was a good-looking kid—close-cropped blond hair, intense green eyes, huge grin. He seemed completely at ease in the company of adults, laughing at our jokes, throwing in his own one-liners amazingly recalled from TV shows and movies. Tomorrow, we'd find out what he could do on the river.

Jackson and I had started canoeing the year before on the Eno and the upper Haw. He was impatient with long stretches of flatwater, wanting instant gratification like so many of his generation. So we moved on to the Lower Haw and ran every rapid, including Gabriel's Bend.

Though I did most of the steering, Jackson seemed to be a natural in the bow. He responded to my commands with quick, agile moves, leaning out to plant his paddle as if he'd been doing it for years. He liked whitewater and said he wanted to try bigger rapids. This kid was ready for the Nantahala.

"It's going to be a full weekend trip," I told him. "We'll be camping out at night and running the river during the day. It's not dangerous, but we could tip over in a few places."

Jackson seemed to contemplate that last statement. "Will we have enough to eat?"

In the darkness surrounding our campsite, a dozen fires glowed. Car doors slammed; laughter rose and fell. This wasn't the wilderness experience I preferred, but it comforted Jackson. On previous camping trips, he was constantly waking up, imagining bears and burglars just outside the tent. This night he slept soundly.

At first light, we piled into Roger's van and headed to the River's End Restaurant next to the famed Nantahala Outdoor Center. The retail store was closed at this hour, and the parking lot virtually empty. We asked for a table by the window so Jackson could have a view of Nantahala Falls. Instead of a thundering flume, the falls was reduced to a pile of dripping rocks.

Like many rivers in the Southern Appalachians, the Nantahala is turned on and off over the course of the week by a hydroelectric plant that uses the streamflow to power its turbines. During World War II, the Tennessee Valley Authority dammed rivers all across the region to provide cheap electricity for aluminum smelters in east Tennessee. These days, the hydroplants feed into the larger electrical grid and are used to provide power during periods of peak demand—typically late morning though early evening on weekdays. Other times, the floodgates are closed and the water stored up behind the dam.

The damming of rivers for hydroelectric power has been a mixed blessing for canoeists. It destroys the natural flow of the river and confines paddling to a predetermined schedule. But on days the plant is running, you're guaranteed to have plenty of water. Saturday is a "scheduled release" day on the Nantahala. And that's a money day for the dozen or so commercial rafting outfitters that run the river, as well as private boaters like us.

We finished breakfast and walked out to find the street clogged with traffic. School buses loaded with rafters spat and groaned around the curve in front of the restaurant. Men and women with river tans and sinewy bodies streamed in and out of the outdoor center.

Back at camp, I hurried Jackson through his morning chores. "Get your paddling clothes on and brush your teeth. The river starts in twenty minutes."

"Jeez, Dad, take it easy."

"And don't forget to go to the bathroom."

The parking lot at the put-in was jammed. Herculean guides stood atop buses tossing rafts onto the pavement. Clients garbed in lifejackets and helmets gathered in noisy clusters on the lawn. Next to these college-aged students and adults, Jackson looked impossibly small. He stood alone in his too large quick-dry shirt and helmet waiting for us to unload the boats. But I couldn't wait for them to see what he could do on the river. We would show these people how to paddle a canoe.

This would be the inaugural run for my Dagger Caption, one of a new breed of canoes introduced in the 1990s and specifically designed for whitewater. These "playboats" were shorter than traditional touring canoes—twelve or fourteen feet long as opposed to sixteen or seventeen feet. They had "rockered" hulls, bowed up at the ends to make them easy to turn. Seats had been replaced by foam saddles with thigh straps to snug the paddler in tight. And every square inch not needed for seating was taken up by air bags designed to keep the boat riding high in the event of a capsize.

It had taken me awhile to warm up to these new boats. I'd watched canoes go through changes in material—wood-and-canvas to aluminum, aluminum to composite plastic. That was fine with me. But when they came out with canoes shaped like a banana and painted Dayglo orange, I felt truly offended. The Caption was the prettiest of the lot, slightly rockered and colored powder blue. Having tested one on the Nantahala the year before, I knew it could perform.

The put-in for the Nantahala was a garage-sized boat basin built just off the bank. We carried the canoes across the parking lot and took our place in line.

Jackson frowned. "How come there aren't more canoes?"

I surveyed the assortment of watercraft—kayaks, rafts, and "duckies," inflatable kayaks with open cockpits. There were only a handful of canoes.

"Rafts are better for people who don't have a lot of experience," I said. "They're real stable, and they bounce off of rocks. I don't like them 'cause they're hard to steer and slow on flatwater. Duckies are fun, but you're sitting in water half the time."

"How about kayaks?"

"Kayaks are cool. They're more maneuverable than canoes, and they don't take on water. But you have to learn to roll, which I've never done. Besides, I like paddling with other people."

I didn't tell Jackson, and hated to admit it to myself, but canoes—even the newer models—were becoming scarce on whitewater rivers. Younger paddlers were all going to kayaks and duckies. Canoes were too stodgy for this new generation.

We slid our boat in the water and settled into the saddles. I tightened the straps around my thighs and blew some extra air into the flotation bag. Keith and Roger came behind in the yellow canoe, George and Michael in the Freighter.

As we paddled into the swift current, the Dagger yawed upstream. Jackson grabbed the gunwales.

"Don't do that," I said. "Always keep hold of your paddle."

"We were about to tip over, Dad!"

"No, we weren't. This boat feels tippier than our Explorer, but it holds on edge real well. You'll see."

We turned downstream, caught up in a sea of moving boats. Raft guides jockeyed for position, hurling mock insults at their cohorts. Canoes banged off rocks. Duckies spun in circles. I'd seen crowds on the Nantahala before, but this was ridiculous.

If you can disregard the human hordes, the Nantahala is a beautiful river. Hemlocks hug the rocky shore, long, low branches reaching just above the tips of the waves. Drawn from the bottom of a deep lake, the water is cold—fifty-three degrees year-round—and clear enough to see bedrock six feet under. On summer mornings a mist hangs over the river so thick you can hardly see the boaters in mid-stream. As the sun clears, the high mountain ridges ("Nantahala" means "land of the noonday sun"), the mist burns off to reveal a shimmering surface.

"Patton's Run coming around the bend." I kept my tone serious but not threatening. "You're going to see a pillowed rock right in the middle of the river. Aim left and brace through the waves."

We rounded the bend to find a canoe broached on the rock, its bow sticking right in our path.

"Draw right!"

Jackson pulled hard, the sinew flexing in his thin arms. The bow angled in, slipping through the narrow gap between the boat and the shore. We punched through the tail waves and eddied out behind a mid-stream rock.

"Good job!"

Keith and Roger came around the corner, dodged the canoe, and swung in behind us.

"We would've hit that boat if we hadn't seen you boogey for shore," Roger said. "Way to go, Jackson."

Keith nodded his approval. I glanced away to hide a sudden tear.

As we negotiated the Nantahala's many wave trains, I admired how the Caption handled. It rose to meet the waves instead of plowing through them like my old canoe. If the waves were higher on one side, I found I could deflect the spray by leaning the boat to the opposite side.

"Don't tilt it too far, Dad."

Around every bend, we overtook pods of rafts and duckies that had launched before us. Canoes might have their shortcomings, but speed wasn't one of them. I felt as if we were flying across the surface, leaving the rest of the world in our wake. Jackson was growing more confident by the mile, tireless in his paddling, though it might have been me who was driving the hardest. Even our friends were falling behind.

"You need to slow down and keep the rest of us in sight," Keith admonished as we waited in the eddy below Delebar's Rock.

"Sorry, man. I forgot."

In its sixth mile, the Nantahala straightens out, paralleling a railroad track on the north shore. One of my favorite memories from childhood is of steam engines—black behemoths belching smoke and steam, pistons flying, drivewheels spinning. I assumed that these were gone forever, like the otherworldy dirigibles that sometimes drifted past our house. It was too much to expect that one might appear in the midst of this exhilarating run, yet above the rush of water, I heard an unmistakable huffing.

Around the bend came a Baldwin locomotive, its silver-nosed boiler and single headlight bright against the shadowed forest. The engine pulled a line of coaches bearing the moniker of the Great Smoky Mountains Railway. Tourists leaned through the open windows, waving at the man and boy in the powder blue canoe.

I threw down my paddle and waved with both arms.

"Dad!" Jackson yelled. "Keep hold of your paddle."

Crushed by my son's disinterest, I watched the engine disappear around the bend, its pulsating breath soon lost to the rush of the rapids.

The river began its winding descent toward Nantahala Falls. A patch of well-worn ground appeared on the south bank marking the path used to scout the rapid. I told Jackson at the outset that we would make our decision whether to run the falls when we got to this point. We pulled over and waited for the others.

George stepped out of his boat and wrapped Jackson in a burly arm. "My butthole always tightens up when I get to this point. How 'bout you, Jackson? Feelin' a little runny?"

I loved the way George acted with Jackson. His humor was as sympathetic as it was outlandish. Jackson grinned in affirmation. We headed down the trail.

The overlook to Nantahala Falls is always crowded on Saturdays. Bystanders and boaters perch on the rocks and wooden viewing stand, cameras and camcorders held high. Their cheers and jeers tell the fate of boaters running the falls. I found an opening along the guardrail and pulled Jackson in beside me.

Nantahala Falls is more like a pour-over than a falls—a ten-yard-wide chute over a sloping rock ledge. But the approach is tricky. The river sweeps around a bend and through a hole above the falls. You can miss the hole by hugging the inside of the bend, but that puts you above the steepest part of the falls and a standing wave that can stall or flip you over if you don't have the right speed or angle.

I pointed out the best route to Jackson. "We want to stay to the left of that hole. As soon as we pass it, draw the bow toward the right. I'll try to line us up going over the falls. When we hit that wave, paddle like hell."

We watched a trio of kayakers surf the wave below the falls, doing enders and three hundred sixty degrees. A pod of rafts ploughed through, clients cheering as they bounced over the drop.

"Whaddya say, Jackson?"

"Let's watch a few more."

Just as we were about to leave, a group of boys paddling a small raft drifted into the hole above the falls. The raft momentarily stalled, disgorging one of its passengers out the back. While his buddies paddled blithely onward, the boy spun in the hole, eyes and mouth forming circles of mute alarm.

A wet-suited figure leapt into the pool and grabbed the boy by his lifejacket. With a few swift kicks, he brought him safely ashore. The crowd clapped, and the parade of rafts resumed.

Jackson frowned. "I don't know about this, Dad."

"Don't worry," I said. "I can get us past that hole."

Nantahala Falls is not a killer. I would never have encouraged Jackson to run it if I thought there was more than a remote possibility that he would get seriously injured. Over the years, thousands of people have gone through this rapid with only a handful of drownings. But there was a fifty-fifty chance we would flip going over the falls and have to swim to shore. If Jackson went in that frigid water, maybe banged his shins on a rock, his feelings about canoeing might change, and not just for this trip. I'd seen how he reacted to minor injuries on the soccer field. He was slow to get back in the saddle if he went back at all. I had to keep that boat upright.

"You guys gonna do it?" Keith asked.

I glanced at Jackson. "Yeah, we're going."

"I'll get my throw bag."

Once more in the boat, I went over the route with Jackson. "And when we hit that wave at the bottom ..."

"I know. Paddle like hell."

Jackson hated swear words. It pained him to use one even in imitation of his father. I gave him a hug and settled into the stern. "Which side do you want?"

"Right. I already told you."

"O.K. Let's do it."

We pushed off and rode the swift water around the bend. The current pulled us faster than I wanted. Was that the hole we just passed? Helmeted heads of kayakers loomed above a break in the waterline. The falls!

"Draw left," I shouted.

The wave rushed at us. We hit at an angle.

"Paddle!"

The canoe jerked sideways, pitching Jackson halfway over the gunwale. I countered with a low brace, paddle pressed flat against the surface. We hung in the balance, rolled at a forty-five-degree angle. Then, as if a hand reached up from underneath, the canoe rocked back to level.

A cheer went up from the crowd. Jackson grabbed his head. As a good canoeist must do, I put the moment of fear behind me. We'd made it through the Falls. That was all that mattered for now.

Chapter 11
The Pigeon

Ever since that first day I crossed the Blue Ridge Mountains on my way to Chapel Hill, I held a dream. I imagined that somewhere in the folds of those wooded hills, a river lay undiscovered. Not by the locals of course, but by the masses of paddlers that now crowded the Nantahala and Chattooga. A small river, hissing over beveled ledges shadowed by hemlock and beech.

At first, I was alone in the dream, paddling with a notebook in my shirt pocket on which to name the many rapids. Then, it was Cathy and me, sitting on a shallow ledge, our legs stretched out in the sun. When I started canoeing with Keith and the guys, they entered the dream as well. I wanted everyone I knew and loved to share in the magic.

The year before we married, Cathy and I drove to meet her parents at their family farm in Knoxville, Tennessee. We followed Interstate 40 west of Asheville, North Carolina, through a winding gorge that cleaves the northern edge of the Smoky Mountains. I guessed there was a river at the bottom of that gorge, though it remained hidden beneath a thick canopy of trees.

Just past the Tennessee line, the interstate crossed the gorge. I angled toward the shoulder, craning to see over the bridge rail. The mountainside fell away to a dark ribbon of water streaked with beards of white. Rapids! Lots of them!

The mountains gave way to foothills. A billboard appeared beside the highway where the river crossed under. "Pigeon River Just Ahead, Polluted by Champion International. Lord Help Us, EPA Won't."

Back in Durham, I asked Howard DuBose at River Runner's Emporium about the Pigeon. Howard snorted. "Damn right it's polluted. It gets sucked into Champion's paper mill in Canton and comes out black as tar and smelling like rotten eggs. North Carolina refuses to crack down on the mill because they don't want to lose the jobs, so Tennessee's trying to get the EPA to step in. They won't move either, assholes."

"How long has it been like that?"

"Since 1908," Howard said. "The year they opened the mill."

I laughed at the irony. 1908 was the year my father was born. "What about the rapids? Looked like some nice ones."

"Supposed to be Class III-IV whitewater through the gorge, but no one wants to go near it. Besides that, C.P.&L. has a dam and hydro plant at the top of the gorge, and they cut off the flow when they aren't making electricity. They refuse to tell the public when the plant's going to run. Who wants to drive five hours to find the river dry?"

Howard's message all but killed my hopes for the Pigeon. Yet I couldn't shake my curiosity. Each summer as Cathy and I traveled back and forth to Tennessee, I drove ever closer to the rail, stealing glances of the river through the trees.

Then, in 1989, a break. Under constant pressure from the State of Tennessee and citizens groups like the Dead Pigeon River Council, the EPA agreed to step in and impose stiffer requirements on the North Carolina mill. They ordered Champion to lighten its wastewater discharge to meet a monthly average of fifty color units—roughly the color of ginger ale— where the river crossed into Tennessee. And Champion promised to install equipment to reduce the sulfurous smell. Champion announced half a billion dollars in plant improvements to be started within the year.

Meanwhile, C.P.&L's license for the Walters hydroelectric plant came up for renewal. A new federal law required that recreational interests be considered along with power generation needs as a condition for awarding a license. Rafting outfitters in Tennessee demanded regularly scheduled releases of water, similar to what was practiced on the Nantahala and Ocoee.

The winter of 1992, I called officials in Tennessee and learned that Champion had already brought some of its new systems on line. Color was lightening, and odor was down. But, no, the official said, nobody was running the river, nor did he know of any plans in the offing. "The Pigeon's been polluted since 1908," the man told me. "Some reputations die hard."

I began to see a window of opportunity. There would be a period of time, maybe a year or two, when the Pigeon was clean enough to run, but not yet recognized as such by the boating public. I could be the one to rediscover the river, or rather I and my friends.

That spring, I argued for taking our annual trip to the Pigeon. Keith was unmoved.

"Why would we want to run a polluted river?" he asked.

"I'm telling you, man, it's getting better. And what's a little stink for the chance to discover someplace new?"

The following winter, I got word that an outfitter named Jerry Taylor had moved to the riverside town of Hartford, Tennessee, in anticipation of starting a commercial rafting business on the Pigeon. I phoned Jerry and introduced myself, then asked him about the condition of the river.

"It's a little funky," Jerry said, "But nothing that'll kill you."

Would he be willing to guide me and a group of friends down the Pigeon in the spring?

"Sure thing, dude. Y'all can stay with me."

I relayed the news to Keith and the guys. They agreed that if what Jerry said was true, they were willing to give the Pigeon a try.

That spring, we loaded the canoes onto the trailer and headed to Tennessee. Hartford was one of those towns you normally blew by on the interstate without a second glance. The lone gas station closed at 9 p.m. The general store/post office didn't even have a lighted sign. I got the feeling that the locals had just as soon you didn't stop.

Jerry lived in a ramshackle house sandwiched between the interstate and the hacked-off face of a mountain. We wrestled the van up the pot-holed driveway and parked next to an aged school bus. Jerry was waiting on the porch, bushy-haired and shirtless, his wiry six-foot-four-inch frame leaned against the railing.

"Is this O.K.?" George called out the passenger-side window.

"Suits me," Jerry said.

"I wasn't sure if it was assigned parking."

Jerry caught the glint in George's eye and smiled as he ambled down the steps. "I'd invite y'all inside, but there ain't nothing in the way of furniture. You'll probably want to pitch your tents out back."

We followed Jerry around to the back yard, a triangular piece of ground sheltered by the mountain on one side and woods on the other.

"Mind if we build a fire?" Keith asked.

"No problem, dude. Just pull some of the branches off that dogwood."

"How about rocks for a fire ring?" I asked.

Jerry pointed to a stone border surrounding an old flower garden. "Use those for all I care. I'm just rentin'."

We set up camp and began preparations for dinner. Inspired by our industriousness, Jerry fetched a can of gasoline from a shed and poured it on a brush pile at the back of the yard. As the flames roared skyward drifting hot ashes onto our tents, Jerry admired his handiwork.

"This is great, y'all," he said. "I've been meaning to do this for months."

Keith proceeded to cook one of his signature meals—blackened chicken with wild rice and asparagus, flavored this night with ashes from the brush fire. We pulled an extra folding chair out of the van and invited Jerry to join us. As Keith handed him a steaming plate, Jerry's eyes widened.

"Damn, you guys know how to eat!" he said.

I asked Jerry to tell us about the Pigeon.

"It's a kick-ass river," he said. "Seven Class IIIs and one Class IV. 'Course, it depends whether there's any water in it or not. FERC is supposed to issue that license for the Walters Plant sometime this year. If they give us scheduled released at least five days a week, this place'll be hoppin'."

"Anything in the water that might make us sick?" Roger asked.

"Not unless you plan on drinking it." Jerry said.

Michael uncorked a bottle of Chardonnay. "What's the plan for tomorrow?"

"Walters should be crankin' up about 10 AM," Jerry said. "They've been running about forty megawatts—a little low for my taste, but it'll make some waves."

"What are we talking about, one-to-two-footers?" George asked.

"Hell, you say. Three-to-four-footers at least."

Roger laughed. "Jerry, you don't know who you're dealing with. Three-foot waves are more than enough to do some of us in."

Jerry sniffed. "You hard boaters," he said, using the rafter's term for canoes. "You need to get you some duckies. They'll ride right over that shit. Got a couple extra if anyone wants to try."

Michael sat up. "I might be interested in that. George, do you mind if I leave you to paddle the Freighter alone?"

"Anything to lighten the load," George said.

In truth, we were all coming to realize that paddling the shorter solo canoes was the best way to tackle pushy rivers. Tandem boats were too hard to maneuver and took on too much water. Keith and Roger had purchased solo boats shortly after I did (the Caption was capable of carrying two paddlers, but was better suited for one). We'd been urging George and Michael to do the same.

Next morning, we gathered on the front porch while Jerry pulled two uninflated duckies out of his stack of five and plugged in his pump. "I'm pretty sure these'll hold air," he said.

Jerry strolled over to the school bus and threw open the back door. "Stick your boats in here. We'll leave your van in town."

"You're going to use *the bus* to carry five of us to the put-in?" Keith asked.

"Sure, dude. Gotta keep it cranked for my customers."

Jerry hopped behind the wheel, and the engine roared to life. An impish smile crossed George's face.

"Hey, Jerry, I've got a present for you," he said.

George dug into the glove compartment of the van and produced a little round floating compass attached to a suction cup. He walked around to the front of the bus and pushed the object onto the hood.

"Now, you know which way you're going!" he said.

George's gift set the mood for the trip. We joked and hollered as we rumbled up the interstate— "Which way now, Jerry?"

Exiting at Waterville, we wound downhill on a crumbling two-lane highway and bounced onto an old cement bridge. The Pigeon rolled out from underneath, solid whitewater in both directions. I turned to Keith with a smug grin. "See, man? What did I tell you?"

The put-in lay in the shadow of the Walter's hydroelectric plant, a handsome turn-of-the-century brick building with tall mullioned windows and pedimented "quoins." At its base, a dark, sulfurous brew flowed from beneath three cavernous arches.

"Whoo, boy," George said. "I'll need to wash my clothes tonight."

"You'll get used to it," Jerry said. "A couple of miles down, you won't smell a thing."

We dragged our boats down the steep bank and started to load the gear. Before anyone else had his lifejacket on, Jerry was in his duckie, surfing the waves below the power plant.

"Hey, Jerry," Michael yelled. "Aren't you gonna tell me how to paddle this thing?"

"Just get in it and go. Best way to learn."

With that, Jerry turned and headed downstream, swept up like a leaf in the wind.

The rapid below the powerhouse stretched a hundred yards and more. Roostertails sprouted all across the surface. White noise rose and fell. Buffeted by cross currents and angled waves, I struggled to follow Jerry's lead. Finally, he eddied out behind a huge boulder in mid-stream.

"Hold on, man," I said. "I've got a boat full of water."

The others arrived, breathing hard, equally in need of bailing. All except Michael, whose duckie had bobbed harmlessly over the waves.

"See what I mean?" Jerry said. "Duckies rule."

Keith glowered. "We'll be sure to wait for you when we hit the flatwater."

"Ain't no flat stretches on this sucker," Jerry said.

Back in the current, we flew under the Waterville Road bridge. I-40 lay just up the mountain, hidden by a wall of trees. I had worried that road noise would mar the experience, but the constant rush of water canceled out the sound of traffic. For all we could see or hear, we might as well have been in a wilderness.

Around every bend, we faced another rapid, another series of obstacles and openings to be deciphered on the run. Just when I needed a break, the Pigeon straightened out, gently stair-stepping to the base of a camel-backed ridge. I pulled over to watch the grand procession—five boats fanned out across the river, sliding and leveling, sliding and leveling.

At the bottom of the run, the walls closed in again. A vein of rock angled in from river left, forcing the current along the opposite bank. What I could see of the rapid didn't look bad, but a rumbling in the distance spoke of trouble. We gathered in an eddy to hear Jerry's instructions.

"This one's a Class IV," Jerry said. "Ride that wave train until you get to that boulder on the right-hand bank, then hang a sharp left."

145

Roger peered downriver. "This doesn't look bad. What makes it a IV?"

Jerry smiled. "You'll see."

Bending his long torso over his outstretched knees, Jerry took off. He turned at the boulder and dropped out of sight. We waited for him to appear on the bank.

"You think he's planning to wave us on?" Keith asked.

Michael laughed. "Who, Jerry?"

Unable to wait any longer, I set off along the right hand bank, just out of reach of the fluttering alders. The bow pitched up and down as the waves grew higher. As I approached the boulder, the sound of the river changed as if a door had opened onto a monstrous, churning propeller. The dark colors disappeared from the river. I plunged into a world of white. Glassy tongues lashed out, threatening to swallow the canoe. All I could do was paddle forward and hope to stay upright. And there in the middle of the rapid was Jerry, paddle whirring as he surfed some impossible wave. I flew past him, glided into an aerated pool, and pulled out on shore.

The big boulder along the bank looked to offer a view back upstream. I scaled its craggy face and signaled the others on with a wave of my paddle. One by one, they fought their way through, grim faces resolving to smiles as they arrived at the bottom. Meanwhile, Jerry was in heaven, turning three-sixties in the middle of the rapid.

"Guys," George said, "We're in the presence of either greatness or lunacy. I'm not sure which."

Downstream, the river slowed as it pooled behind a cleft in the rock. The passage through was marked by two giant waves, whose arching crests sparkled in the noonday sun. I thought to let Jerry run first, but the rapid looked harmless. Rising to the top of the first wave, I stared into a watery hole dark as a well. My canoe swooped downward, turned at an angle, and rose again on the other side. Teetering for a moment on the crest of the wave, I threw in a downstream brace and fell over sideways.

The current slowed to a gentle drift. A few swift kicks brought me to shore, none the worse for having been dunked. My skin didn't itch, and my clothes smelled O.K. I dragged my canoe onto a gravel bar and waved my arms, a warning no doubt undermined by my eager grin. Each successive paddler approached the rapid, eyes wide, paddling stopped, and as his boat cleared the last wave, a huge smile spread across his face.

After dumping the water out of our boats, we decided this sunny gravel bar was a good place for lunch. I set my soda in the river to cool, noted the color of the water. It looked about like ice tea, not much different from the Haw. That may not have been good enough for the Dead Pigeon River Council, and no doubt it was darker up near the mill, but at this time in this place, it didn't bother me.

After lunch, Keith paddled out to play in the waves. I leaned back on my elbows, stared up at the cloudless sky. We could stay here all day and never see another person. This was it. This was my dream.

"Say, Jerry, has anybody named these rapids?" I asked.

"Somebody named the IIIs and IVs a few years back. This one's Roostertail."

I sniffed. "Roostertail. That's kind of anti-climactic. Are these names published anywhere or are they just local lore?"

"Nobody's published anything that I know of."

"So you could print your own map. Call 'em anything you want."

Jerry shrugged. "I suppose. I've been meaning to print up a map for my customers."

I glanced around. "Whaddya think, guys? What's a better name for this rapid?"

George stroked his goatee. "How about Big Fucking Hole?"

"Yes, Big Fucking Hole!" Roger said.

Jerry shook his head. "Come on, dudes, I can't print that on a map."

"Okay, then, BFH," George said.

Jerry nodded. "That'll work."

I sat up and breathed the wild mountain air. We were making history. Years from now, people would ask where the name of this rapid came from. Guides would tell them, "Some guys from Durham named it. They were the first ones down here ..."

Below BFH, the Pigeon became more of a drop-pool river. Still, these were big rapids, perfect for duckies and rafts. Jerry was going to make a killing out here if he could get his business together.

We pulled out at the town of Hartford and headed over to the general store. The old lady behind the counter gave us the evil eye as we came through the door—a bunch of city slickers talking loud and wearing strange clothes. As I examined the meager selection of white bread, toilet paper, and Vienna sausage, Roger whispered in my ear, "Dare I ask for a cappuccino?"

Back outside, I took a bite of my stale candy bar and pointed out to George the empty lot beside the river. "This is where it's all going to happen," I said. "Outfitters' stores, parking lots ... How long do you think we have?"

George glanced down the empty street. "I figure another year, maybe two."

We came back to the Pigeon the following spring. Jerry had bought the general store and was doing double duty as check-out clerk and guide for the Smoky Mountain River Company. The water quality of the Pigeon was steadily improving, and C.P.&L. had agreed to regularly scheduled releases to start the following year. Fortunately for us, the public had yet to discover the river.

"Let me ring these people up; then we'll get paddling," Jerry said. "Anybody know how to change the ribbon on this fucking cash register?"

Waiting outside in the parking lot, I noticed that the compass was gone from the hood of Jerry's bus. George was philosophical.

"Some things just aren't meant to last," he said. "By the looks of it, old Jerry's got his hands full with other stuff. If you ask me, he's not cut out for retail."

Back on the river, Jerry was a happy man. He bombed down Powerhouse, stopping at the big rock to let the rest of us catch up. He surfed the micro-eddy in the middle of Lost Guide and the curling wave on Vegematic. As we paused for lunch on the gravel bar beside BFH, I marveled that we still had the Pigeon—and Jerry—to ourselves.

"Another year, and you're going to be booked solid with paying clients," I said. "You won't have time for us."

Jerry shook his head. "Nah, I'll always take time off for you guys."

"Hey, what happened to the map? Did you ever print one up?"

"Just a hand drawn thing, but I'm making photocopies of it. It's got your rapid on it, George—BFH. Folks around here are already calling it that."

George slapped Jerry on the back. "You're a good man, Jerry. Just for that, I'm going to give you one of my baloney medallions."

For me and my friends, paddling the recovering Pigeon was becoming an annual spring event. I only worried that Jerry would become so busy with his business that he wouldn't be able to run the river with us. But I always assumed that he'd let us camp in his back yard and join us around the campfire with a beer or a joint in hand. The dude would abide!

When I called the store in the spring of 1995, a woman answered the phone.

"Is Jerry around?" I asked.

A long pause followed. I could feel the drop coming.

"I'm sorry to tell you this," the woman said. "Jerry's passed on."

My head spun. "He's dead?"

"Yes, sir. He was riding a horse across Big Creek Bridge. It was raining, and the horse must have slipped and fallen. They found Jerry lying on the rocks."

* * *

It was another two years before I could return to the Pigeon. This time, I came with my family—Cathy, Jackson, our daughter, Allison, and a passel of cousins. We were all in Knoxville for the annual Murphy family reunion. The kids were eager for adventure. I suggested a raft trip down the Pigeon.

From the moment we arrived in Hartford, I could see everything had changed. Billboards beckoned the public to come raft the Pigeon. Outfitters had taken over the abandoned school house. A giant cinderblock boat barn claimed the lot by the river. School buses topped with rafts jammed the narrow streets.

Our trip with Wildwater Adventures was scheduled for 3 pm, but the girl behind the counter informed us that the 1 o'clock trip had gotten stuck in traffic on I-40 and was running about an hour late. She urged us to look around the gift shop.

I thumbed through the post cards and T-shirts emblazoned with the predictable "I Survived the Pigeon River" monikers. I asked the clerk if they carried any maps of the Pigeon.

"No, but there's a T-shirt that's got the names of the rapids on it," she said.

She came out from behind the counter and began sorting through the rack. "Here it is."

I took the shirt and held it up to the light. Powerhouse, Lost Guide, Roostertail ...

"What happened to BFH?" I asked. "Isn't Roostertail called BFH now?"

The girl blanched at my sudden display of emotion. "Not that I know of."

I handed her back the T-shirt and stomped outside. What happened that the name was changed back? Did Jerry never print a map? Was his word not taken as gospel?

I returned to the counter. "Did you know Jerry Taylor?" I asked the girl.

"No, but I heard of him. There's a plaque for him on Big Rock."

"The one right below Powerhouse?"

She nodded. "You'll go right by it on your trip."

"That's great. I'll be sure to look for it."

Back at the boat barn, the previous trip arrived, and we were ushered out the back door to "the briefing area." Without any introduction about the river, Mike, our strapping young guide, launched into a lecture on safety procedures. "Don't put your foot under the center thwart, or someone could fall against your knee and break your leg," he said. "Don't let go of your paddle handle, or you're likely to knock someone's teeth out. And if you fall out of the raft, don't ever try to stand up in the river, or you could get your foot caught under a rock and drown."

Allison pulled on my arm. "Dad, I'm not sure I want to do this."

"Don't worry," I said. "You'll have a blast when we get out on the river."

From a dripping pile left by the previous trip, we picked out helmets, paddles, and life jackets. We boarded the bus with twenty other people and crowded into the seats. Staring at the pasty-faced clients with their chubby legs and small hands, I felt a sudden urge to cry. I was a canoeist!

At the put in, we took our place in line behind half a dozen rafts. Mike gave out our seating assignments. "Mom, you take the back right next to me," he said to Cathy. "Dad, you're back left."

We carried the boat to the river and climbed aboard. As we pushed out into the river, Mike gave us our last-minute paddling instructions.

"When I say forward left, everybody on the left hand side paddle forward. When I say back right, everybody on the right hand side paddle backwards. Got that?"

"Yes."

"I can't hear you."

"Yes!"

As we approached the top of Powerhouse, the air vibrated with a familiar roar. I braced myself for the cross-currents that had buffeted my canoe. Nothing. The raft slid forward smooth as a hearse.

Allison glanced at Cathy with a relieved grin. I turned to Mike. "So what does the Dead Pigeon River Council say about the river these days?"

"Who?"

"The Dead Pigeon River Council?"

"I don't know about them."

"Well, what do *you* think of the water quality in the Pigeon?"
Mike stared at the river. "Seems okay to me."

Suddenly, there was Big Rock and right near the top, a small bronze plaque shining in the sun.

"There's Jerry's plaque!" I said. "Can we stop and take a look?"

I stabbed my paddle into the river, tried to slow the lumbering raft. But Mike had no time for reminiscence, and in a moment, we were past.

Chapter 12
The Chattooga Revisited

The rain started around midnight, a scattering of thumps on the tent fly that soon became a steady downpour. I listened to Jackson's breathing in the sleeping bag next to mine. At least he could sleep.

Somewhere down in the valley, the Chattooga was rising. At two feet on the Highway 76 gauge, the big hole would start to form on the rapid above Sandy Ford. At two-and-a-half, the Narrows would wash out. What the river would be like beyond that level, I had no idea.

After the Nantahala, Section III of the Chattooga was the logical next step for me and Jackson. I felt confident we could make it down everything except Bull Sluice, and that we could walk around. But that was at "normal" springtime water levels. Even before we had left Durham, the Chattooga was running higher than normal. And now this.

I knelt inside my down cocoon, head in hands. Where should I draw the line and cancel the trip? How could I know whether I was leading my son on a grand adventure or disaster? I begged for an answer, but heard only the wind and rain.

At first light, I backed out of my sleeping bag and donned a rain jacket and pants. Outside, the woods lay shrouded in fog. The kitchen tarp sagged under its load of rainwater. Without thinking, I pulled down on the edge and caught a blast of cold water in the face.

Keith emerged from his tent and rummaged through the cooking gear until he found the coffee pot.

"So what're you thinking about the river?" he asked.

"Don't know. Thought I'd go down to the bridge and check the gauge. Want to come?"

"No, thanks. I'll get breakfast going."

I drove out to the paved road and clicked on the radio. The weatherman was calling for clearing skies and temperatures in the low seventies. Good news.

At the bottom of the hill, I pulled onto the shoulder and stared at the water swirling beneath the bridge. Definitely high. I decided that if the gauge reading was three feet or above, Jackson and I weren't going. I slipped down the muddy trail and found the white metal bar poking out of the water. It read two feet eleven inches.

The rest of the crew was up by the time I returned—Michael, Roger, and two new "members," Charlie and Randy Humble. The Humble brothers grew up in east Tennessee, canoeing the Nolichucky and the Ocoee. Section III of the Chattooga was a cakewalk for them, especially for Randy, a top-knotch kayaker. When I relayed the news about the river level, Randy just shrugged. Charlie, a canoeist, was a little more circumspect. "Is that too high for you and Jackson?"

"I don't know. I've never done it at this level."

"We've got some good paddlers here," Charlie said. "We can always bail you out if you get into trouble."

I glanced at Keith. "How about you?"

"I'm definitely going. It's supposed to be a nice day."

Michael voiced his approval. Roger was silent.

I missed not having George along. His back had been giving him trouble, and he'd reached the point where he could no longer paddle. I begged him to come to the Chattooga, offered to mount him on his canoe like El Cid, but he was adamant in his refusal. If he were here now, he'd say something to lighten the mood. Instead, we stood around with eyes downcast.

I weighed the options—Jackson and I could sit around camp all day and wait for the others to return; drive five hours back to Durham; or trust that we could make it down the river with a little help from our friends. I roused Jackson and explained the situation.

"Whatever you think is best," he said.

Most fathers pray for the trust of their thirteen-year-olds. But we can't know everything. Our judgment is not always to be trusted. I took a deep breath. "Let's do it."

With the promise of a sunny day, I urged Jackson to wear only his quick-dry shorts and shirt under his rain jacket and pants. But as we stepped out of the van at the trailhead to Earl's Ford, a chilly wind blew beneath an unbroken raft of gray clouds. We lowered the boats from the trailer and started dragging them downhill.

"How far to the river?" Jackson said.

"About half a mile."

"Half a mile!"

We reached the clearing and set the boats at the water's edge. This was Jackson's first look at the Chattooga—silent and swirling here at the start.

"This doesn't look too bad," he said.

"Yeah? It gets tougher farther down."

As the rest of us loaded the canoes, Randy jumped into his kayak, paddled out to midstream, and practiced rolling. Kayakers are a different breed—lone wolves—versus the social animals that gravitate toward canoes. I sensed that Randy wasn't much aware of or concerned with our limitations. But I trusted he'd help out if any of us got in trouble.

I put the canoe in the water and dropped into the rear saddle. As Jackson sat down in the forward position, my heart sank. I couldn't see a thing past his helmeted head and shoulders. In the year since we'd last canoed, Jackson had grown a half a foot taller. He might be scrawny for a thirteen-year-old, but he was plenty big for this boat.

As we set off from Earl's Ford, I found I could see downriver if I held the canoe at an angle. This would work as long as we were on flatwater, but I would have to straighten out once we got to the rapids.

War Woman appeared on the horizon—the first of the named rapids on Section III. Right off, I noticed a funnel-shaped wave blocking the chute down the top ledge. Michael, paddling out front, blithely took the wave head on and flipped upside down. He bobbed to the surface, wide-eyed and sputtering, and kicked back into his duckie.

"We need to stay away from the middle of that wave," I said to Jackson. "There's less curl closer to the rock."

"I see it."

Jackson drew the bow to the right. As we slipped past the wave, a watery hand reached out and yanked the stern sideways. Adrenaline shot through my veins. My heart was still pounding when we eddied out at the bottom.

157

Roger followed our line and came through upright. But his deep set eyes were caves of worry. More and more, as we tackled tougher rivers like the Pigeon and the Chattooga, Roger's smile was giving way to a frown. Keith and I worried aloud that his skills were falling behind ours, that it was only a matter of time before he got into trouble. Still, he insisted on coming, and we were not about to turn him away.

Beyond War Woman, the Chattooga picked up speed. Nameless rapids grew into daunting wave trains. We dodged left and right, trying to avoid the haystacks, but water poured over the gunwales and sloshed around the hull.

Jackson moaned, "My feet are soaked."

"Wiggle your toes. Keep 'em warm."

I spotted a giant boulder on river left and realized we were in the middle of Rock Garden. We normally drifted through this stretch, admiring the spectacular rock formations. But today, the current pulled us along at a runner's clip. I made a feeble attempt to divert Jackson's attention, pointing out the leaning slab we called Stonehenge, but his eyes were on the bend ahead.

As if opening a door onto a crowded room, we emerged from behind the boulder to the head of a roaring rapid. The boat angled downward and started to buck. I leaned out to see ahead, and suddenly we rolled upside down. Ice water closed over my face. I broke the surface and caught my bearings. Jackson was just ahead of me, the boat to one side.

"Keep your feet up!" I yelled.

Waves broke over my head—three, four, five, six.

"Head for shore!"

I rolled onto my side and started kicking, paddle in one hand, stern line in the other. It was crazy trying to swim like this. Two yards from shore, I tried to stand. The canoe swung at the end of the rope and pulled me off my feet. I kicked again, grabbed a root dangling from the bank, held on.

Randy peeled in from midstream and drove the canoe onto a sandbar with the nose of his kayak. I scrambled along the bank and grabbed the water-filled boat. Jackson crawled out and stood shivering on the bank.

"Help me with the canoe," I said.

"I can't. I'm freezing."

"Just stand there doing nothing, and you're sure to warm up."

Jackson stomped his foot, his scrunched eyes on the verge of tears. I couldn't believe I was doing this now. Why couldn't I find the right words?

Keith arrived and helped me flip the canoe.

"I can't see a fuckin' thing in this boat," I said. "Jackson's gotten too big."

Keith nodded. "It's tough."

With the boat secured, I turned back to Jackson. He had yet to move from his spot on the sandbar, possessed now by the cold. I put my arm around him and rubbed hard.

"This wasn't your fault," I said. "You were doing fine."

Making up was hard for me. It wasn't something the Manuels did easily. We were much better at harboring grudges. My son was not that way.

"So what happened?" he asked.

"I don't know. I leaned out to try to see the rapid."

"Don't do that again."

I said nothing more. There was no way we would make it down this river by running the rapids blind. An experienced bowman could call out the route, but Jackson wasn't ready for that. It dawned on me then that Jackson might never be ready tackle whitewater on his own, that he was really here to please me. What had I gotten him into?

We dropped back to the middle of the pack and managed the next few bends without incident. In the distance, jets of spray danced above the water line—Dick's Creek Ledge. We pulled up to the big scouting rock in mid river. Its flat surface was all but submerged, leaving just enough room for seven of us to stand.

"Are you sure this is Dick's Creek Ledge?" Michael said.

"It's Dick's Creek," Keith said. "But it's a fucking waterfall."

The serpentine route down the double drop on the left was a maelstrom of cross-currents and roostertails. The pillowed rock in the middle threw off a geyser six feet high. The ledge to river right, normally dry enough to walk across, was now a roaring spillway.

"Looks like the right hand side is the only way," I said.

Charlie frowned. "I don't know. The bottom looks pretty squirrelly."

While the rest of us huddled like ducklings, Randy jumped into his kayak and paddled straight down the left-hand channel. In one perfect motion, he launched off the pillowed rock, soared a dozen feet through the air, and landed upright and paddling at the bottom of the ledge.

Roger shook his head. "Your brother's got balls, Charlie."

The longer I looked at this rapid, the more frightened I got. "Jackson, I'd suggest you walk this one," I said. "Hop in, and I'll put you on shore."

"Are you gonna run it?"

I nodded. "The ledge looks runnable to me."

As we pushed off the rock, Charlie called after me. "Which route are you going to take?'

I pointed at the ledge.

"Where exactly?"

I shrugged.

With Jackson safely on shore, I paddled into the still water above the ledge. The sheer drop hid the landing zone, but I kept a mental image of what looked from the scouting rock to be the safest route. I paddled to the edge and held my breath. The bow pitched downward. I hit and leveled out. Piece of cake.

How is it, I wondered, that obstacles that appear so daunting often turn out to be easy, while the unnamed threats do us in? That's the way it often is with rivers. Many a great paddler—men and women who have survived the most horrendous drops—have bought it on a simple Class III. Maybe they weren't paying attention. Maybe the sheer number of Class IIIs they run means the odds of dying on one are greater. Or maybe, as the fatalists say, it was just their time.

I waved my paddle in the air, signaling the others to follow my route. Everyone landed upright, surprised as I was at his good fortune. Even Jackson sounded upbeat when I reached him onshore.

"I could have run that, Dad," he said.

"Yeah? We'll do it together next time."

Beyond Dick's Creek, the hillsides closed in, and the gradient increased. Rapids came back to back, their steady roar drowning out our shouted commands. The river forked around a wooded island. Charlie dropped into a hole and emerged with a boat full of water. I angled the canoe for a better look.

"Dad, what are you doing?"

I hurried to bring us back in line. Too late. We hit the hole still at an angle and started to roll. For an instant, everything hung in the balance. Jackson leaned out over the gunwale. I held my paddle overhead. This can't happen again, I said. I won't let it happen. We hit the water.

When I surfaced this time, we were moving at a dead run. A fallen tree lay halfway across the channel. I yelled at Jackson to get away. He started to swim, grazed the jagged end and spun free. Just as I slipped past, the canoe slammed into the trunk and pinned.

Another drop loomed ahead. I swam for the island, clawed at the rocks until I found one I could hold. Randy flew past in his kayak, chasing after Jackson.

"Grab the stern loop!" he yelled.

With Jackson clinging onto the rear, Randy paddled hard for the island. They made it to the shallows where Jackson let go and tried to crawl onto the rocks, but his elastic cuffed pants, ballooned up with water, held him down.

Keith and Charlie ran their boats ashore.

"I've got Jackson," Charlie said. "Help John with the boat."

Keith and I scrambled back up the bank until we got to the fallen tree. The boat was pinned ten yards from shore with the bottom facing upstream, a good sign in that water was not pouring into the hull. From either end, bow and stern lines fishtailed in the current. If we could reach one of those, we might be able to pull the boat loose. Randy charged upstream in his kayak, but the current was too strong. Somehow, we'd have to reach the boat from shore.

I glanced at the tree—an old loblolly that had broken off about ten feet above the ground. The trunk lay at a forty-five-degree angle, its battered crown stuck in the raging river.

"If you'll give me a rope to hold onto, I'll crawl down there," I said.

Keith frowned. "You sure you want to do that?"

"I can get down all right, but I might need help getting up."

Randy arrived with a length of rope, which he lashed around the broken stump. I wrapped the rope around one arm and laid myself across the trunk. It felt solid, rough. I wasn't going to slide off. Sliding backwards, I eased down the trunk until my feet touched the canoe. I kicked at the hull. Nothing. I lowered myself and kicked again.

"Fucker's pinned tight," I said.

Keith pointed at the rope trailing out from the stern. "Can you get ahold of that?"

I glanced down. No way to reach it with my hand, but I might get it with my foot. I dangled my neoprene bootie in the current and hooked the underside of the rope. Twice it fell off. The third time, it stayed.

"Gimme some tension!"

Keith pulled on the safety rope, and I started scrunching my stomach, inching upward like a caterpillar. An arm's length from the bank, I handed the stern line to Randy. He gave it a yank, and the canoe swung free. Charlie grabbed the boat as it drifted to shore.

"How's it look?" I asked.

I stepped onto dry ground and headed down the bank to check on the boat. Keith and Charlie blocked my path.

"You and Jackson need to get off the river," Keith said. "Sandy Ford is just around the bend. You can pull out there and hike up the trail."

I stared back. No one had ever told me to get off a river.

"You don't want this to be the last time Jackson ever canoes," Charlie said. "If you flip again, that could do it."

Jackson huddled on the shore, lips blue, shaking from the cold. They were right. I had no business even thinking of going on. "How do we get back to camp?" I asked Keith.

"You can hitch a ride when you get to the road. If not, it's only a couple miles back to the put-in. I'll give you the keys to the van."

I relayed the news to Jackson, explaining there was a takeout just around the bend.

"I'm not getting back in that canoe," he said.

"Jackson, we're on an island. We have to paddle off."

I ushered him to his seat, promised once again we would not tip over. But there is no bargaining with a river. Within seconds of pushing off, we were back in the whitewater. We hit a rock, spun three hundred sixty degrees. Jackson grabbed the gunwales.

"Get me off!" he wailed. "Just get me off!"

Finally, the rapids subsided. A sandbar emerged on river left. I drove the canoe onto the bar and jumped out to hold it fast. Jackson stepped on shore, wiped the tears from his eyes.

"We made it, buddy," I said.

The rest of the crew pulled in beside us. Hands reached out to pull the boat ashore. We rolled it over and drained it out.

"I guess we'll see you this afternoon," Keith said.

He held out the keys to the van, a medal of defeat. I knew this was the right thing to do, but the sight of my friends gathered in their boats, heading off without us, was almost more than I could bear.

Then, Roger stepped out of his canoe.

"You know, I've had enough of the Chattooga for today," he said. "I think I'll hike out with John and Jackson."

"You don't have to do that," I said.

"No, I want to."

I fought back the urge to hug him. No doubt, Roger was worried about his own safety. But he was doing this for us, too, for me and especially for Jackson. Out of all the people present, including myself, Roger was the one guy who knew what my son was feeling.

As the others headed down river, Roger gave them a wave. "We'll have the beer on ice when you get back to camp."

"Thanks for helping me," Jackson said. "You guys saved my life."

I smiled at Jackson's comment. He wasn't really in that much trouble. Then the thought of what could have happened began to sink in. A couple of inches to the left, and he would have been pinned between the tree and the canoe. If he'd tried to stand in the fast water, his foot might have been trapped, and he'd have drowned in seconds. Bad things happen quickly on rivers.

I slung the bowline across my shoulder and started up the path. It was a hard slog, the canoe straining behind. Every step, I thought of what would have happened if I'd lost him. I *had* lost him as a canoeist, of that I was sure. He would never paddle whitewater again. But we would go back to camp and light a fire. We would sit in a circle with the other men and tell the story of a boy and his foolish father.

Chapter 13
The Ocoee

Keith and I floated in an eddy at the bottom of Surfing Rapid on the Tuckasegee River, getting ready to ride the big wave. He'd already done it once, ferried into midstream until he reached the watery hand that held his canoe in place. Now it was my turn.

The surfing hole was maybe forty feet away, nothing that a competent canoeist couldn't reach. I paddled out of the eddy aimed upstream and started to work my way across. The river came at me, unrelenting. As I neared the hole, my stroke faltered. What if it grabbed me and wouldn't let go? What if it drew me in? The current pushed the nose around, and I hurried back to the eddy where Keith sat watching.

"You suck at ferrying," he said.

Twice more, I tried to ferry to that hole, and twice more, I failed. We ran the rest of the river without incident, but for days thereafter, I stewed about Keith's comment. I didn't need to be an expert at ferrying to get down these rivers. Roger and Michael would never even attempt such a move. But the fact that I couldn't do something that was well within my grasp bothered me.

And there was more. Keith and I hadn't worked together for years, but every now and then, he let slip a comment about my less admirable behavior back at the office—my tendency to bail out of difficult tasks, to trash my boss behind his back. Sarcasm and subterfuge, those were my weapons for dealing with complexity and authority. Out on the river, there was no hiding my inadequacies.

So, I called the Nantahala Outdoor Center and arranged for a private lesson. Not on the Nantahala, a river I had long ago mastered. I wanted to go over the mountains to the Ocoee.

The Ocoee River—the big one, a non-stop rollercoaster that pushed the limits of canoeists and kayakers alike. Keith had run it years before, and though he managed to come through unscathed, he confessed to being terrified most of the way down.

I was willing to take the lesson alone, but decided to invite Keith to join me. Having another person along would boost my courage. And however it turned out for me, I wanted Keith to know that I'd tried.

We headed to the Nantahala on a Friday afternoon. After setting up camp, we drove to the Outdoor Center to check out the latest equipment. It was all kayaks now, a new generation of squat little boats that looked like flattened clogs, designed strictly for playing in the rapids. The notion of running a river from beginning to end was passé. People were in it just for the thrills.

I picked up a guidebook on the Ocoee and brought it to the counter.

"Gonna kayak the bad boy?" the clerk said.

"Nope. Canoe."

He raised his eyebrows. "Good luck."

Until that point, I kept my fear in check. I avoided thinking too much about Keith's descriptions of head-high waves and hydraulics that would roll you half a dozen times before spitting you out—Maytagging, the book called it. Now, my nerves started to tingle, fires lighting in my back and neck.

Years before, my friend Annie had told me a story of how her husband had fallen out of a raft on Section IV of the Chattooga and gotten caught in a hydraulic. While the others watched helplessly, he spun in circles unable to escape. He drowned within minutes. Even then, the river would not give him up. A rescue team was forced to cut down a tree and float it through the rapid to knock him out. Lying in my tent the night before my lesson, I became Annie's husband, forever in the river, forever drowning.

A dog barked in the pre-dawn darkness. I crawled out of my bag and headed for the wash house with a bad case of the runs. The toilet seat was cold, the air foul. I thought of Cathy, Jackson, and Allison at home warm in their beds. Thank God, I hadn't dragged Jackson in on this venture. This was my river to cross.

At first light, Keith and I drove down to River's End Restaurant and ordered their French toast special with coffee and bacon. I couldn't eat it.

"You sure you're ready for this?" Keith asked.

I nodded without conviction.

"You need to eat something."

We paid our bill and stopped in a convenience store where I bought a couple of bananas. Maybe I could keep these down. After another trip to the bathroom, I donned my river clothes. We drove to the Outdoor Center to meet our instructor.

Bob Beasley was maybe fifty years old, with wire-rimmed glasses and a receding hairline. He moved in an unhurried manner, shook our hands and offered an even smile.

168

"So what have you guys done before?"

I blurted out the names—Chattooga, Pigeon, Nolichucky.

Beasley nodded. "You'll do fine."

On the hour-long drive to the Ocoee, we traded the usual river-running stories. Keith's enthusiastic recounting of our exploits buoyed my spirits. By the time we reached the river, the knot in my stomach had eased off.

The put-in for the Ocoee was a madhouse. School buses crammed the parking lot above the dam. Hordes of rafters clustered with paddles in hand. Like the Nantahala, the Ocoee is a dam-controlled river, and on those days when water is being released, boaters converge from all over the Southeast.

The sight of people carrying their boats to the put-in got my adrenaline running. I was eager to get on the river. Instead, Beasley ushered us to the lake behind the dam.

"We're going to do about an hour of warm-ups here before we hit the river. John, I want you to paddle a straight line about thirty yards out, turn around and come back."

Lake paddling? This was bullshit. I was here to paddle whitewater. I slumped into my boat and took hold of the paddle. If Beasley wanted a straight line, I'd give it to him.

Using my best J-stroke, I set off down the lake. Beasley called after me. "Don't use a J stroke; use a pry."

I glared over my shoulder. "What's wrong with the J?"

"The J is fine for flatwater, but it's too slow for Class IV rapids. You need short strokes that will instantly adjust your direction."

I shook my head in disgust. At Keewaydin, we laughed at the kids who used a pry with its jerky, indelicate motion. It was a sign of poor instruction or none at all.

"Now, turn around and come back on the other side," Beasley said.

I switched hands and paddled on the left. Beasley frowned again. "Don't let go of the paddle. You need to learn to paddle on both sides without changing grips."

"I've never had trouble switching grips."

Beasley shook his head. "The half-second it takes you to change hands is a half-second you may need to get out of trouble. And every time you let go of the paddle, you run the risk of dropping it. You can't afford to do that on the Ocoee."

It felt awkward to paddle with my forearm extended across my stomach. I couldn't keep the boat in a straight line.

"Keep trying," Beasley called.

Meanwhile, Keith, who'd learned canoeing from God knows who, was earning nothing but praise. I'd seen him use these strokes out on the river, but considered them showboating.

Beasley called the practice to a halt. We pulled our boats onshore and ate lunch on the tailgate of his car. By now, the parking lot was quiet, the rafters gone downriver. So much for getting ahead of the crowd.

The put-in for the Ocoee is awe-inspiring, even for experienced boaters. Water thunders over a thirty-foot-high dam and surges through an impassable boulder field on the near side of the river. The open channel lies a hundred yards out, requiring a ferry across the runoff at the base of the dam.

Beasley knew about my poor ferrying skills and offered to show me a "cheat route" along the near shore. My goal for the day was to learn the things I'd shied away from, but I followed him through the boulders like a penitent child.

We gathered in the eddy of the aptly named House Rock and surveyed our next move. Below us, a sloping ledge with a menacing hydraulic stretched halfway across the river. This time, there was no cheat route. Beasley gave us the basic instructions for ferrying to the far side of the river. "Come out of the eddy at a ten-degree angle. Take short strokes and use a pry to make any corrections. John, you come after me."

Moving with seemingly effortless strokes, Beasley ferried across the river until he reached the open channel. Keith gave me a nod.

"Go get 'em, John."

I paddled out from behind the rock and started to work my way across. The current rushed beneath the hull. I countered with urgent strokes. Halfway there, I started to panic. My arms began to tire. I wasn't making progress. Desperate to close the distance, I increased the angle of my ferry. The current grabbed hold of the hull and pushed the nose around headed toward Grumpy Ledge. I hurried back to House Rock and Keith's wagging head.

"Don't say anything," I said. "I can do it."

There comes a point when you grow tired of the way you are. Something clicks in your mind, and you know it's time to change, to become a stronger person. When I came out from behind House Rock the second time, I held my line. I worked the boat across the river, resisting the temptation to increase my angle. When I reached the open channel, I turned and bobbed through the waves. Beasley was waiting in the eddy.

"Better."

Keith made it across with a visible sense of relief.

"Don't ever ask me to do that again," he said.

We caught our breath, then turned and headed downstream. An unguided paddler would have a rough time on this river. The maze of boulders and ledges defied easy scouting from above. Kayakers were scattered all over the river, surfing in holes, scooting down narrow passages. You could follow the rafts down the main channel, but they were a hazard in and of themselves, blocking the view downstream, knocking smaller boats aside.

Deftly moving between boats and boulders, Beasley led us through Gonzo Shoals and Broken Nose. We "boofed" the ledge beside Double Suck, sliding sideways over the dry lip and splashing down in the pool beneath.

Just downstream, the Ocoee narrowed and dropped through an enormous wave train. Double Trouble was twice the size of BFH on the Pigeon.

"Best way to run this is to hug the right side and duck out of the wave train as soon as possible. If you get stuck in the middle, keep paddling. John, are you ready?"

My heart pounded against the ribbed front of my life vest. I glanced at the shoreline, considered how easy it would be to walk around Double Trouble. I pushed off and drifted to the edge of the sloping funnel. Too late, I saw that I was dead in the middle.

The canoe slid down the incline and up the face of the first wave. The bow teetered on the crest, pivoted to the left.

"Paddle!" Beasley called.

I pried furiously, trying to straighten the canoe, crested the second wave and slid down again.

"Keep paddling!"

I hit the trough at an angle and began to roll. The water rushed at me. And then I was under.

The first thing I noticed was the color—blue-green with millions of bubbles suspended above and below me. We were all moving together, like souls in space. And the sound, a muffled roar, soft and distant. *Get to the surface!* I stroked upward, burst into daylight, saw a wave about to break, and ducked down again. *Better down here. Just surrender and drift.*

The waves subsided, and I rose to the surface, the noise fading behind. I rolled onto my back and stuck my feet out in front. Beasley's mango-colored canoe appeared beside me.

"You all right?"

"Yeah. Water's warm."

"You kind of drifted out in the middle."

"Happens a lot," I said.

Beasley smiled and headed off after my boat. Keith arrived and told me to grab onto his stern.

"Jesus Christ, I thought you were a goner. You disappeared after the third wave."

"I'm cool, man."

We paddled down to where Beasley held my boat pinned against the shore. I hauled the Caption onto the rocks and drained the water out.

"Let's take a break," Beasley said. "I've got some drinks."

I stripped off my life vest and laid it on the sloping granite. Keith dropped down beside me and held out a juice box.

"So, what do you think?" Keith asked.

"About the river? It's great."

"Serious?"

"Yeah, man. It's just what I needed."

Keith slapped me on the back.

I stared back down the path we'd just traveled. Sunlight sparkled atop the waves in mid-channel and the smooth, copper-colored boulders along the edges. Beyond lay the road winding around a steep hillside, thick with oak and pine.

Shouts rose above the rush of water. A trio of kayakers bobbed through Double Trouble. They moved like water bugs, scooting into the eddy, then back into the waves to surf and spin. When they'd had their fill, they passed along the near shore. One of them, a woman with long, blonde hair, looked our way.

"Beasley! Is that you?"

She spoke with an Australian accent and, drawing near, flashed pale blue eyes and a gorgeous smile.

"What are you doing here, man?"

"Giving these guys a canoeing lesson."

"Canoeing, eh? I'm quite impressed." Turning to me, she asked, "Has there been much carnage?"

I laughed at her pronunciation—"cahnidge." Most likely, this was a common expression among the hardcore river runners on the Ocoee. I thought about my humiliation at the lake, my botched ferry at Grumpy Ledge, my capsize on Double Trouble. But in retrospect, they didn't amount to much.

"No. Not much carnage," I said.

"Well, carry on. One big Daddy left."

A mile downstream we came to the big Daddy—fifty yards of roaring, head high waves, white-tipped and jagged. Tablesaw was the most intimidating rapid I'd ever seen. Before today, no one could have convinced me that you could run it in an open canoe.

"Best way to take this one is right down the middle," Beasley said. "You'll need to ferry out to get in position. John?"

I stared at the waves descending into chaos. "Straight down the middle?"

Beasley nodded.

I moved to the edge of the eddy. A twenty-yard ferry would put me in midstream. Anything less would be disaster.

Two forward strokes, and I was out in the current, water racing beneath the hull. *Easy, now. Don't panic.* I worked my way into mid-channel. Another stroke for good measure. *Now turn.*

The current grabbed the nose and swung it around. I leaned downstream, my paddle braced flat against the swirling waters.

The canoe shot down the incline and up the face of the first wave. Paddle and pry, paddle and pry. White spray flying overhead. Paddle and pry, paddle and pry. Down up, down up, down up. Still paddling, still paddling. Waves subsiding, noise fading, fear melting. Fear melting. Hissing, hissing. Gone. I shipped my paddle and drifted.

* * *

Later on, the evening I came back to visit my dying father, after Mom left the room, I got up and took Dad's hand. I sat on the bed and looked into his face. Dad's eyes were closed. He couldn't speak. But I understand that you can hear right to the end. I told him that he'd been a good father. I told him not to worry, that I'd learned well the lessons he'd taught me—how to navigate, how to spot the rocks, to find a river and always be near it. I didn't say that I loved him. And when he died a few hours later, I didn't cry. But I believe I was on the right river and am on it still, just a few bends away from where it pools behind a hemlock-shaded ledge and spills into white.

Postscript
The Cuyahoga

In December 1974, Congress passed Public Law 93-555, creating the Cuyahoga Valley National Recreation Area. The recreation area was designated as the Cuyahoga Valley National Park in 2000. The park encompasses 33,000 acres and draws more than three million visitors a year, making it the seventh most visited national park in the country. The main attractions are the Ohio & Erie Canal Towpath (now used as a bike path) and the Cuyahoga Valley Scenic Railroad, both of which parallel the Cuyahoga River.

The Cuyahoga River through the park remains polluted, though not nearly as bad as in the 1970s. The river looks and smells normal for much of the year and even supports springtime runs of steelhead trout. During periods of heavy rain, Akron's Combined Sewer Outflow still poses a threat to the river. The city's long-term plans call for upgrading the sewage treatment facilities to be able to handle peak flows. Until that happens, the Park Service does not recommend canoeing or kayaking the river.

The Pigeon

The Pigeon River in Tennessee has become one of the most popular whitewater rafting runs in the Southeast. Half a dozen outfitters carry approximately 70,000 customers down the river each year, adding hundreds of thousands of dollars to the Cocke County tax revenues. Jerry Taylor's Smokey Mountain River Company was taken over by his daughter following his death, but has since shut down.

In 1999, Champion International sold the pulp and paper mill in Canton to its workers, who formed Blue Ridge Paper Products, Inc. The mill continues to make improvements to its production processes, though nothing as dramatic as the major modernization of the 1990s. Water quality in the Pigeon is much better than it was prior to the modernization. Water color is still an issue, especially during periods of drought when the relatively high volume of effluent from the mill turns the river notably darker.

The plant's North Carolina wastewater discharge permit comes up for renewal every five years. In hopes of forcing stricter color requirements, groups such as Clean Water for North Carolina and the American Canoe Association have requested that the EPA intervene in the permit renewal process. The EPA has so far declined to do so.

Photo by Cathy Murphy

About the Author

John Manuel grew up in Gates Mills, Ohio, and graduated from Yale University and the University of North Carolina at Chapel Hill. He now lives in Durham, NC, with his wife, Cathy. John has been a freelance writer since 1990, the majority of his journalistic stories being published in *Environmental Health Perspectives*, *Canoe&Kayak* and *Wildlife in North Carolina*. His short stories and creative non-fiction have appeared in the *Savannah Anthology* and the *New Southerner*. John is the author of another non-fiction book, *The Natural Traveler Along North Carolina's Coast*, and a novel, *Hope Valley*.